Becoming Mama

A Holistic Doctor's Guide to Thriving in Your Post-Baby Body

MICHELE BREZINSKI, M.D.

Two Penny Publishing
1209 SE 21st Avenue
Cape Coral, FL 33990
TwoPennyPublishing.com
info@TwoPennyPublishing.com

For permission requests and ordering information, email:
info@twopennypublishing.com

Paperback: 978-1-965341-05-6
eBook also available

FIRST EDITION

For information about this author, to book event appearance, or media interview, please contact the author representative at: info@twopennypublishing.com

Two Penny Publishing is a partnership publisher of a variety of genres. We help first-time and seasoned authors share their stories, passion, knowledge, and experiences that help others grow and learn. Please visit our website: TwoPennyPublishing.com if you would like us to consider your manuscript or book idea for publishing.

For Ashton and Tyler,
Mama loves you as big as the sky

Table of Contents

Introduction

When you're pregnant, you are flooded with health and medical information on a whole new level compared to anything you've previously experienced. Most of that information doesn't even come from your doctor's appointments. There are thick, technical books like *What to Expect When You're Expecting* and thin, humorous books like *A Girlfriend's Guide to Pregnancy.* Your doctor will give you handouts, and your friends and family will offer advice and send you articles.

Then there's technology. Once you start creating baby registries and looking at information online, your ads and inbox will be flooded. There are more than 50 different pregnancy apps for your phone, and that's just where I stopped counting! You can do online groups with women who share a similar due date, groups for women who are interested in raising their babies a certain way, and local care providers who want to offer you the latest, greatest options at a premium price. At no time in our lives have women been so completely inundated with information about our bodies.

Until the baby is born. Then the waterfall suddenly slows to a trickle, and you've got... nothing. Don't get me wrong, you're still flooded with information. But the information is all about this amazing, wonderful, tiny person you grew and gave birth to—not about you. It's easy to understand why. If you've never raised a child before, suddenly having a little one to take care of can be scary.

But one of the cardinal rules of motherhood is that you can't take care of anyone else if you don't take care of yourself. It's like the emergency demonstration on the airplane before you take off. Put on your own oxygen mask before assisting others. Admittedly, many women, myself included, struggle with putting their own needs first. It's counterintuitive for the "nurture" side of our personalities. Part of what you'll learn in this book is how and why self-care is important. You will also learn what self-care looks like and how other mamas make it work.

The lack of post-delivery information about your own body isn't surprising, however. A woman's body immediately after giving birth is not exactly glamorous. There's excess skin, exploding breasts, lumps and bumps, noises and drips, and all sorts of things we would rather crawl in a hole and tolerate than discuss with anyone. You don't call up your friends because you're freaking out that you just peed yourself because you had a coughing fit in the checkout line at the grocery store and couldn't hold it. Although, I'll make the argument that you should, the point is that our social norms in this country make certain topics "taboo." Historically, a woman's body after childbirth has been one of those topics. I want to change that.

If you received this book as a gift and you haven't yet given birth to your first child, a lot of what I'm saying probably comes as an unpleasant surprise. But before you start to worry too much, I'll offer a glimmer of hope. I gave birth to my first son at age 40, and I walked out of the hospital in non-maternity jeans. Admittedly, they were baggy jeans, and they were exchanged for a pair of sweatpants as soon as I got home, but after toting around a basketball belly for the last three months of my pregnancy, I wanted to look like a normal person for a few minutes. It didn't last. I can probably count on one hand the number of times I put on jeans over the following two months.

A lot of women have shared that tug of war feeling, caught between wanting to be like their pre-pregnancy selves and wanting to just do nothing. What I hear even more commonly is the lack of comfort with our new bodies. Things don't look and work the way they did before, and suddenly there's a lot of uncertainty about what's okay and what isn't. This book is here to help with that.

So without further ado, let me introduce myself. My name is Michele, and I'm a family medicine physician and a proud mama of two energetic little boys, both of whom were born after my 40th birthday. Not exactly how I'd do it again, but the combination of my chosen profession and personal health issues, including being diagnosed with Lyme Disease in my mid-30s, kept me from having kids at a more typical age. Even though I was physically fit, pregnancy was still hard on my body. It was even harder on my mind and my self-esteem as I dealt with all the changes my body and life underwent.

One day, when my younger son was about a year old, my chiropractor, a fellow mama and friend, and I were talking and laughing about the memories of life in the days and weeks immediately after delivery, and she said, "You should write a book about this!"

Full disclosure: I was already in the process of writing a book about something else, and I wasn't sure I really wanted another book. But the idea stuck in my head like one of those little sticker burrs caught in your favorite hiking socks. This book could be a fun book, a place where women could come without fear of embarrassment or judgment. I remembered my own frustrations at trying to find information about different postpartum issues after my first son was born. There was a *need* for this book. And so "Becoming Mama" was born…

This book is designed and written so that you can use it in a variety of ways. You can read it straight through in the last few weeks of your pregnancy or shortly after delivery so that you have an idea of what to expect. One reason I wrote this book was because the constant flow of information about the changes happening to my body dried up after delivery. Most pregnancy books have one teeny chapter at the end about life after delivery, typically about hemorrhoids and breastfeeding. That's not enough.

You can choose to read the chapters out of order and turn straight to whatever information you need, like a "choose your own adventure" novel. Each chapter stands alone, so you can go right to where the answer to your question is located and get the information you're looking for—fast. If you're looking for knowledge, I've got you covered with trustworthy information written in plain, everyday language that you can understand and relate to. If you're more the doing type, look for the toolkits at the end of the chapters for tips and suggestions you can use right away. Or if you're up at 2:00am feeding your baby, exhausted and discouraged, you can just skim through and read the stories at the beginning of the chapters and scattered throughout. These stories are from real women like you. They will make you laugh, cry, and feel not so alone anymore, because 2:00 am feedings can get lonely, too.

There's something about the middle of the night. I used to love working the night shift at the hospital, with the peace of the dimmed hallway lights. But the night can be lonely. It can give increased weight to sadness and fears. You're not alone, Mama. I hope this book helps you realize that and helps you talk about what you're experiencing with your loved ones and your doctors.

So, what's your story? Are you pregnant or already immersed in life after having a baby? Do you have one child or more? Did you just deliver, or are you picking this book up months, or even years later, because your body never returned to normal and you want to know why? Or are you here for an entirely different reason? If you want to connect with more articles and information about women like you, please check out the book's website at: www.becoming-mama.com. I'd love to hear your story, too! In the meantime… happy reading!

Santa Claus Belly

"One morning, about a week after my son was born, I was slouching on the sofa in a nursing sports bra and a pair of yoga pants. I was sipping a cup of coffee after breastfeeding my son, and he was asleep on the sofa against my side. He stirred and flung his little arm out, and it hit my stomach. My whole stomach shook—it quivered and jiggled. I chuckled, and to my surprise, it shook again. In a sense of morbid amusement, I smacked the area lightly with my hand and watched as all the tiny folds and wrinkles of loose skin started to jiggle around, like one of those Jello desserts at a church potluck. Oh my gosh! I have a Santa Claus Belly! I think I actually said it out loud. I had one of those basketball pregnancies, the kind where you carry your baby all sticking out in front, so I had a lot of excess skin. And when I moved or laughed or something bumped it, that skin took on a life of its own. I remember taking a video of it, watching my belly wiggle and jiggle and shake with a mix of laughter and horror, and wondering if my stomach would ever again resemble the flat, toned belly I'd been so proud of pre-pregnancy..."

—The Author

So, I'm happy to report that I no longer have a "Santa Claus" belly. It went away gradually over the next few weeks. I don't remember exactly when it hit the point where things no longer resembled a Jello dessert, but I promise it did happen. Granted,

I certainly don't have a "flat, toned belly," but that's a story for another chapter. So, why does skin behave that way? What gives it the ability to bounce back like that? Can you speed up the process?

What is skin anyway?

Let's start by talking about skin, because there's a lot more to it than what we see looking at the surface of the body from the outside. Skin is actually made up of three distinct sections: the epidermis, the dermis, and the hypodermis. In case you didn't guess, "derm" means skin.

The epidermis, the part on top, is what most of us think about when we talk about our skin. But even the epidermis has layers with nearly dead cells on top and special cells on the bottom layer that are always dividing and growing more skin cells. There are four layers in the epidermis in most of your body, and an extra fifth layer over the palms of your hands and the soles of your feet to make them thicker and better able to stand up to frequent contact with other surfaces.

Did you know that your skin replaces itself entirely about once a month? When you put on lotion, it affects mostly the epidermis, providing a little moisture to the upper layers. This is why all lotions contain water. It also helps seal the surface of the skin to prevent further loss of body water. This is why all lotions also contain some type of waxy ingredient.

Although the epidermis is what we all associate with the word "skin," it's the dermis, that middle layer, that plays a key role in getting rid of excess skin after delivery. This layer consists of fibers, fat cells, hair follicles, and nerve endings. The fibers are mostly two specialized proteins called collagen and elastin. It's these proteins that give skin shape and structure. Decreasing collagen under the skin as you age is also a big part of what causes wrinkles.

You hear about collagen all the time in the beauty industry and, more recently, in Paleo diet circles. There are actually five different types of collagen. Two types are found in the skin, but there is also collagen in your bones, muscles, tendons, hair, and the organs of your body. One special type of collagen even helps to make up the placenta. Collagen's main job is to give structure to the otherwise gloppy dermal layer, providing a scaffolding of sorts in which everything else is suspended. As we age, collagen levels naturally decrease. This is one of the main reasons that skin starts to sag.

Elastin, however, is the real star in making Santa Claus belly go away. Elastin, as the name implies, is the stretchy elastic fiber running through the scaffold that collagen supplies. Some elastin is thin, like the little skinny elastic bands we use to pull our hair back, and some is thick, like the waistband of your maternity leggings. The thin elastin bounces back more quickly, but the thick elastin is stronger. To see how elastin works, simply pinch a fold of your skin and then let go. The skin rapidly goes back to its original shape. The reason for that is elastin. After your baby is born, you no longer have a tiny human stretching out the skin of your belly. Elastin responds to that loss of stretch and starts pulling your skin back together.

Elastin fibers are connected to each other by chemical bonds. As your belly starts to stretch with baby's growth, the old bonds are broken, and new ones are formed and reformed based on the new degree of stretch. After you deliver, those new chemical bonds are suddenly no longer "right" and your body has to start revising their location again in response to the lack of stretch. This doesn't happen overnight, and the structure gets revised multiple times over the coming days and weeks.

Looking beyond the skin, the walls of the stomach, also known as your "abs," play a role in helping Santa Claus belly disappear. They remodel into shorter versions of themselves once they are no longer being constantly stretched by your baby. We will talk more about abdominal muscles later in chapter five.

What about stretch marks?

Stretch marks are one of the most dreaded side effects of a baby's rapid growth inside of you. Medically termed "striae distensae," some women get them on their belly during pregnancy or on their breasts during early breastfeeding. On a cellular level, they behave like injury and scar formation under the skin. They originally appear as pale pink, often itchy areas. Then they morph into deep reddish-purple lines, and finally, they usually fade to white with time. Medical researchers aren't exactly sure what they are or why some people get them. We know that they are more likely to appear during periods and areas of rapid growth, and we know that they're associated with high levels of steroid hormones (e.g. estrogens, testosterones, and stress-induced hormones). In pregnancy, you get both rapid growth and high estrogen levels. Stress can also be a huge factor when it comes to stretch marks. It is hard not to be stressed out at some point during your pregnancy, so it's no surprise they're fairly common.

So why do some women, even women like me with basketball pregnancies during the pandemic, not get stretch marks? Based on studying women with certain inherited diseases, we know that there is definitely a genetic link to getting stretch marks. That link has to do with the genes that tell your body how to make collagen. When researchers look at skin that gets stretch marks under a microscope, they see that it has less gene expression for collagen and another protein called fibronectin.

We also know that they are more likely to develop in people with liver disease, not typically related to pregnancy, and with decreased immune system function. Although HIV is the classic example of decreased immune function, certain medications, including some medications used in pregnancy, can be another cause of this.

So, once you have stretch marks, what can be done about them?

The unfortunate answer is not a lot. Some research shows that a common acne medication, retinoic acid cream, can help if applied during the early light pink stage. However, this is typically less effective once the marks have darkened and ineffective once they've turned white. Some types of chemical peels and microdermabrasion, used for wrinkles and surface scars, might be helpful. Laser therapy is generally considered the most promising treatment, although effectiveness and safety vary by laser type, and the price tag can be quite steep. Most insurance companies designate laser therapy as "cosmetic", and therefore, do not cover treatments.

Will taking collagen supplements help my abdominal skin?

Maybe. No one has studied collagen supplementation for postpartum issues. The research on collagen supplements, unsurprisingly, has centered on decreasing wrinkles and other signs of aging. However, according to this research, the use of a safe, high-quality collagen supplement does seem to help aging. And one of the big causes of wrinkles is loss of collagen and elastin under the skin. So, it is possible that it may help Santa Claus belly, too. There are a couple of things to remember if you choose to try collagen. First, these formulas are made from animal bones and tissues. If you are a vegetarian, vegan, or an animal rights supporter, this is probably not for you. Second, the supplement industry is largely unregulated. This means the quality and safety of supplements available varies widely, so make sure you do your research and consult a trusted professional before purchasing a product.

Are there other supplements that might help my skin?

Maybe. There are numerous Vitamins and other antioxidants that are known to help the skin in general. Vitamin A (retinol/retinyl palmitate/retinoic acid) is found topically in many anti-aging lotions and other products designed to increase collagen and elastin. As we already discussed, retinoids may help stretch marks. So an "anti-wrinkle" lotion may be helpful and is generally going to be a low-risk option. Taken by mouth, Vitamin A is a strong antioxidant, so it is likely to help your health in general. The biggest concern with Vitamin A is that it can be toxic when taken by mouth in the retinol form. This is because Vitamin A is fat-soluble—meaning that if you take a high dose, it does not dissolve in water and get removed in your urine; it stays in your body and builds up in your fat and other cells. This is okay if your body needs more than it was getting, but dangerous if you already had more than enough. If you choose to take Vitamin A in supplements beyond a multivitamin, make sure that it's in the form of beta-carotene or other carotenoids. These compounds are what give carrots and other orange fruits and vegetables an orange color. They can be converted in the body to Vitamin A, and unless you take massive doses, your body is smart enough to only make what it needs.[2]

The B Vitamins are often found in skin, hair, and nail supplements. Niacinamide (Vitamin B3) has been shown in a lab to help the body make collagen and protein in the skin, as well as improve skin elasticity.[3,4] Because B vitamins compete with each other to be absorbed by the body, I don't recommend consuming very high amounts of just one or two of them, as this can lead to low levels of the others. But, taking a vitamin that has many of the B vitamins and a relatively high percentage of B3 in comparison to the others is typically safe. And using niacinamide-containing skin creams is certainly okay.

Vitamin C is a powerful antioxidant that stimulates collagen production and is also necessary for the production of collagen. It's often part of skin lotions and creams that are advertised to reduce wrinkles and brighten skin. However, the research suggests that it doesn't penetrate into the skin very well when applied as a lotion. Vitamin C can also be taken by mouth and is much more beneficial in this form. In addition to helping the body make collagen in the skin, it may provide other benefits, such as improved immunity. Because Vitamin C is water-soluble, if you take more than your body can use, the extra Vitamin C will be removed from your body in your urine. This is why it is considered relatively safe at reasonable doses. Higher doses above 2000 mg can cause diarrhea, however, and it may also affect breast milk production. One final caveat is that Vitamin C is a very mild blood thinner. If you have any history of blood clots or bleeding, or any prescription medication use or chronic medical conditions, you should talk to your doctor before taking extra.[1,5]

What about food?

As Hippocrates said, "Let food be thy medicine and medicine be thy food." In medical school, I was taught pharmacology and the use of medications to treat health problems. I tried to see it as an art—picking the perfect drug that would best help my patient with all the nuances of effects—but it just didn't resonate with me. So, I pursued training in integrative medicine, nutritional medicine, and lifestyle medicine. I discovered that the one thing that has the single greatest impact on health and well-being is what you put in your body. So, my preferred way of helping the body became to feed it well.

But what kinds of foods? There are numerous dietary patterns out there, and they all claim to have research supporting their effectiveness and safety—usually surrounding things like weight loss, heart health, diabetes, and cancer. These are the current major medical conditions of concern, so it makes sense that this is how they are marketed. But, as I was taught in medical school, you can make a research study show almost anything you want, depending on how you set up the study. Not all research is good science. Look at tobacco and aspartame. There are research studies sponsored by industries that claim that these things are safe to put in your body, even though the vast majority of the evidence says otherwise. Dr. Atkins claimed to have research that his diet would help with heart disease and high cholesterol. Dr. Atkins also died of... heart disease. So when patients ask me what kind of diet I recommend, I tell them to follow the excellent advice of Michael Pollan, "Eat real food, mostly plants, not too much."

For healing, the body needs a relatively higher supply of nutrients—vitamins, amino acids (proteins), and minerals—than it does just existing. For growing a baby, those nutritional requirements are even higher. This means after delivery, your body's supply may be running low if you haven't been eating well. And if you are breastfeeding, your body's increased nutritional needs continue for the months to come. Plant foods, especially fruits and vegetables, tend to have far higher vitamin and micronutrient density than other options.

As noted above, Vitamins A, C, and E are key for skin health and healing. Consuming vitamins in whole foods where they are present in their natural form is far preferable to taking a supplement. Vitamin A in the retinol form can be found in animal products like chicken livers, butter, eggs, and cheese. Vitamin A in the carotenoid form is present in dark leafy greens like kale and spinach and in all of the orange-colored fruits and vegetables. Sweet potatoes, carrots, and cantaloupe are particularly good sources. Foods high in Vitamin C include citrus fruits, kiwi, strawberries, broccoli, and peppers, both sweet bell peppers and hot spicy ones like jalapenos. Foods high in Vitamin E include nuts and seeds, bell peppers, and avocados. Vitamin E, in particular, is more effective when eaten as part of whole foods rather than taken as a supplement.

More important than any one food, however, is a certain "liquid" nutrient — water. Without adequate hydration from within, the dermal layer becomes less plump, which translates into looser, less structured skin. Women who've recently given birth are particularly at risk for mild-dehydration because their bodies have just rapidly disposed of all the extra water they retained during pregnancy to boost circulation to the placenta. Breastfeeding also dramatically increases hydration needs. An underrecognized cause of lower-than-desired milk production is inadequate water intake. So, bottoms up ladies!

Aim for at least half your body weight in pounds each day. If you weigh 160 pounds, that's 80 ounces of water if you're not breastfeeding, and an extra 2-4 glasses a day if you are. If you don't enjoy plain water, try adding a lemon wedge, orange slice, or other fruit to your glass for a bit of flavor. Yes, you'll feel like you're floating away at first. But your body does adjust, and since your body is about 60% water, you may find that you experience numerous "side" benefits to the change, like improved fatigue, better ability to concentrate, and fewer headaches. Most importantly for our current topic, that dermal layer under your skin will be more plump, and the surface of your skin will be smoother and less dry, all of which will help the overall appearance of Santa Claus belly.

Will certain exercises help the appearance of my belly?

In theory, possibly. However, Santa Claus belly is a problem that happens immediately after delivery to a few weeks later. At this point, your body has been through so much. As I noted above, your skin is drawing back together, and so are your abdominal wall muscles. Your abs were stretched out too, and may have split down the middle. These muscles also need time to shorten up from their "cover the baby bump" length. There are a number of reasons I do not recommend doing any typical ab exercises at this point in your postpartum recovery. First, your core is so weak that it can hardly stabilize you for normal activity. Second, most traditional ab exercises increase the pressure inside your abdomen, and this can lead to problems if performed too early after delivery. Third, if you had a cesarean section, you've certainly been advised not to do them so that the incisions in your uterus, skin, and muscles can heal. This is a time for your body to rest and heal.

Is the skin on my belly ever going to look the way it did before I got pregnant?

Maybe. The end results of Santa Claus belly are determined by many factors, some of which you can control and some of which you can't.

The things you can't control (at least not at this point) include:

- Your age (younger = better chance of full resolution)
- How much weight you gained during pregnancy (impacted by belly size and shape)
- How you carried your pregnancy (more spread out vs. basketball)
- If you developed stretch marks

The things you can control include:

- Hydration
- Nutrition
- Ab muscle dysfunction

If that first list makes you want to cry, let me reassure you. I have a friend who is in her late 30s, has had three basketball pregnancies, and a year after her youngest was born, she had incredible drool-worthy six-pack abs. How? She was the queen of the three things she *could* control, and she worked really, really,

really hard. She's also a lifelong competitive athlete and is overall in awesome shape. So, please know that if you are into sports and fitness, recovery to high levels of performance is possible.

I, on the other hand, do not have beautiful washboard abs. I still have a mild split in my ab muscles and a "mom pooch" that no one will envy. But I admit that my commitment to rehabbing my core and to exercise in general took a serious backseat after I had my second baby after age 40 as a doctor in the middle of the pandemic. That was my choice and I made my peace with it, and that's okay, too. Now that my younger son is no longer an infant, I've re-committed to fitness and hopefully, sometime soon, I'll be able to say that I've resolved most of my "mom pooch." Amazing abs? Not that ambitious. Strong enough core to hike, bike, run, and play sports with my little boys? Yup, that's my goal. Do what feels right for you and your life now. Re-evaluate every few months and change your path if needed. It's okay. You're okay.

But I'm done having babies, and I hate my stretch marks and all this awful floppy skin! Isn't there anything someone can do?

Yes, there is. As far as stretch marks go, laser therapy is currently the best available treatment option. The cost will be entirely out of pocket and typically runs in the hundreds of dollars, with the exact cost depending on the number of treatments and size of the area to be treated. Don't expect miracles. Some women do get pretty good results, but most of the time, you get improvement in the 50-80% range.

As far as the excess abdominal skin, for most women, a commitment to eating healthy and daily exercise will be the best long-term solution. When this is not enough, the most effective, albeit most drastic strategy, is to have cosmetic surgery — abdominoplasty — otherwise known as a "tummy tuck." The cost of this procedure is typically in the low thousands and is not covered by insurance. Any surgery involves medical risks, both from anesthesia and from the surgery itself. It also involves recovery time and an incision. This procedure will leave you with a scar. Where that scar is depends on whether you have a full tummy tuck or just a mini one, but there will be a scar. Most full tummy tucks leave you with a scar around your belly button. Most mini tummy tucks leave you with a slightly curved scar on your lower abdomen just below your bikini line. A mini tummy tuck scar is similar to what you'd have with a cesarean section or a hysterectomy. Sometimes, the full tummy tuck will also use a similar but longer incision to a mini tummy tuck. In sum, the procedure will tighten up the appearance of your stomach, but it will leave you with a scar, and you need to make sure you're okay with that. Most women I know who've had the surgery feel the trade-off was worth it and have been pleased with their results, but surgery is not for everyone, and taking the steps below will help you feel confident in your choice.

If you do choose to consider having either laser treatment or cosmetic surgery, please make sure to do your research. Ask your obstetrician and your primary care doctors if there is a provider they would recommend. Talk to friends and neighbors and make sure that you're going to see someone who will take good care of your body and treat you fairly. There are a lot of people out there who prey on women's insecurities about their bodies. Sad but true. This leads to my last suggestion. Please take some time to reflect on why you want the procedure and what you're hoping to gain from it. Talk to your partner. Look at your kid(s) and your body, and remember how you got there. Then, if you still want to proceed, please do. But doing the mental and emotional work dramatically increases the likelihood that you'll be happy with your choice and the outcome down the road. Don't ever let anyone make you feel ashamed about your choice. This is your body and your life — and your journey. Honor what you need to walk your road.

Toolkit

Sweet Potato Orange Soup Recipe

Sweet potatoes are a nutritional powerhouse that are great any time of year, not just whipped and topped with mini marshmallows at Thanksgiving! This smooth, savory soup gets its brightness from a bit of orange juice and zest. You can also top with pumpkin or sunflower seeds for a bit of a crunch.

- 2lb sweet potatoes, peeled and cut into large cubes
- ½ medium sweet onion, cut into wedges
- 2-3c vegetable broth
- 1 orange (for 2 tbsp juice and 1 tsp zest)
- 1 tsp cumin
- 1-2 tsp salt
- ¼ tsp pepper

Toss the potatoes and onion with oil and place on a baking sheet. Mix the cumin, salt, and pepper in a small bowl and then sprinkle on the veggies. Roast in a 400 degree oven until tender and starting to brown (usually 30-45 minutes depending on the size of the pieces).

While they are cooking, zest the orange. If you're not into cooking, this means very finely grating the orange part of the peel. Once you have enough zest, cut the orange in half and squeeze to get your juice.

Once the potato and onion have cooled slightly, add to a blender or food processor with 2c of broth, and the orange juice and zest. First, blend on medium to break up the larger pieces, then medium-high speed until smooth. Add extra broth (a couple of tablespoons at a time) if the soup is too thick for your liking.

Warm up in the microwave or on the stove and add additional salt and pepper to taste. You can enjoy plain or top with crackers, pumpkin seeds, a dollop of cream, or even chopped crispy bacon.

Bone Broth Recipe

Bone broth (beef or chicken) is a popular item in grocery stores thanks to many of the possible benefits for joints, skin, hair, immune conditions, and gut health. These health effects are thought to be due to the high content of collagen, minerals, and certain amino acids that are drawn out of the bones and into the liquid during the cooking process. I've included it in this book because it's often a safer and better tasting way to obtain extra collagen than taking a powdered supplement. It's also a fast and easy task that makes your house smell like homemade soup/stew, which on a cold day is such a lovely thing!

It's important to understand the difference between bone broth and regular broth. Bone broth is made from cooking beef/chicken bones for long periods of time. Regular broth is made by cooking the meat. Bone broth is usually thicker and somewhat gloppy when cooled due to the gelatin released from the bones. Regular broth is still the same consistency as water.

Before you start, you will need to decide: 1) what kind of broth you want to make and 2) what you are going to cook it in—a pot on the stove, crockpot, or pressure cooker (a.k.a InstantPot or similar).

1. Get some chicken or beef bones. The easiest route for this is to fix chicken legs or wings or cook one of those little four-pound mini chickens from the store. If you want beef, short ribs or a bone-in roast are your simplest options. Eat your dinner and then save the bones in the fridge—or if you have a crockpot, proceed immediately to the next step and let your broth simmer overnight.

2. Place the bones in a crock pot or a large stock pot. Cover with water. Add in vegetables to taste. I typically will add about two large or a dozen baby carrots, half an onion, a clove or two of garlic, and a bay leaf (sold in a spice jar at regular grocery stores). You can also add fresh or dried herbs or other vegetable scraps, such as mushrooms, parsnips, broccoli stems, etc., as desired. But be aware that these veggies do impact the flavor of the final product.

3. Cook on low/simmer for 8-12 hours. I typically add a little salt and pepper to taste at the end of cooking, as how much you need will vary.

4. The fun part—enjoy! You can drink/spoon as a broth or use it as a base for nourishing soups and stews. What you do not consume can be refrigerated for up to four days or frozen for up to three months. Be aware that when cool, your broth will become thick.

Choosing A Supplement

For the safety of yourself and your baby, if you're breastfeeding, you should do a little bit of homework before purchasing vitamins or other nutritional supplements over the counter. This is because the supplement industry is not regulated by the government the same way that foods and prescription medications are, so the possibility of supplement-induced negative consequences exists.

If you are breastfeeding, you must discuss all potential supplements with your pediatrician before starting to ensure that they are safe for your baby.

Most of the major supplement brands will be relatively safe because their brand reputation depends on it. Things like NatureMade and Nature's Bounty are good examples because they have internal testing, USP verification, or both.

Choosing a brand or a product that is USP verified ensures that:

1. The supplement contains the ingredients that it says it contains in the amounts that the label states.

2. The supplement does not have toxic levels of contaminants like heavy metals or pesticides.

3. The brand, or manufacturer, follows the FDA (Food and Drug Administration) regulations for safe manufacturing practices (a.k.a sanitary and safe production).

4. The supplement will break down or dissolve within a certain period of time so that your body can absorb the active ingredients, which are the vitamins/herbs/nutrients on the label.

It is worth noting that "store brands" for SAMs club and Costco are USP verified for many of their products. However, it is important to check the label for the amount of the ingredient you're looking to supplement, as the "dose" per capsule may be quite a bit less than a more expensive brand like NatureMade.

Issues "Down There"

"I delivered my first baby late. Like two weeks late. This meant that my husband and I had to attend the wedding of close friends less than two weeks later. I was so mad at myself for promising we'd be there. So there I was sitting in the pew at the wedding, and I shifted my weight, and suddenly it felt like something was poking me down there. I changed positions again and again without relief. Finally, I went to the restroom and gingerly started to feel around. It didn't take a medical degree for me to realize that the offender was one of a row of stitches along the edge of my vagina, where my body had torn as my son was born. And no matter how I sat, if I was all the way upright, those little threads were stabbing me. I squirmed like I had ants in my pants until Monday, when I walked into my doctor's office and begged for someone to take them out."

—Donna, 34, mama of four

How do I know what's normal down there?

Your body in the first days and weeks after a vaginal delivery usually looks and feels a far cry from "normal." Your labia are usually swollen, sometimes even double their usual size, and everything around them is swollen, too. The longer you were in labor and the harder you had to push, the puffier everything is. To add to the issue, the swollen areas often feel different than usual, too.

If you had some tearing in the skin of your vagina or what we call the perineum (pair-eh-NEE-um), your doctor or midwife may have needed to put in a few stitches to draw the skin back together, control or prevent bleeding, and help you heal.

Many women develop hemorrhoids, which are small bulging veins either just inside or outside your rectum. These can occur prior to or during delivery. Hemorrhoids that appear before delivery can be related to enlarged veins, baby taking up space in your abdomen, and/or constipation. Delivery hemorrhoids happen because of the pressure inside the veins created by pushing. Think of them kind of like teeny tiny varicose veins in your butt.

And don't forget the bleeding. For many women, delivery is the longest and most aggravating menstrual period ever. Initially, most women have flow like a heavy-ish period day, and then over a couple of weeks, this tapers to nothing.

What can I do about my hemorrhoids?

If the first thing that came to your mind when I said hemorrhoids was, "Oh, how embarrassing," you're not alone. For some reason, even though almost half of the women who've given birth have hemorrhoids, they tend to be one of the most difficult subjects to discuss. But they can also cause significant itching and discomfort. Rather than suffer in mortified silence, here are a few steps you can take.

Let's start with a quick review of options over the counter. There are a variety of over the counter products that can relieve itching and mild discomfort. These include the well-known Preparation H, which contains hydrocortisone to soothe itching and inflammation. Products like Anusol Plus contain zinc to help heal and protect the thin and tender skin. Even most diaper creams contain zinc, so in a pinch, you can always grab some from your baby's room. Tucks pads contain witch hazel, which is also a natural anti-inflammatory that is very soothing against the skin.

Additional things you can do include using ice packs to ease the swelling and taking sitz baths (see the Toolkit for instructions) to relax the muscles and improve blood flow. Many women also use moistened wipes instead of toilet paper to ease irritation — just make sure not to flush them!

If you tend towards constipation, managing this is crucial to prevent further enlargement or irritation. The best way to do this is through a combination of medications and diet. Your doctor may have given you a prescription for a stool softener during pregnancy or at the time of delivery. If not, you can purchase a common stool softener called docusate over the counter. Probiotics can also be helpful, with most of the research centered around the common lactobacillus and bifidobacterium containing products.

The most commonly known dietary strategy for constipation is increasing fiber intake. A high-fiber diet is definitely effective and important, but it has a few caveats. First, don't suddenly increase your fiber intake by a large amount, as this can lead to worsening symptoms as your body tries to adjust to the drastic change. The target daily fiber intake for women is about 25g—and most of us don't get anywhere near this. For best results, you want to increase by 3-5g each week.

High-fiber foods include fresh fruits and vegetables, beans and other legumes, and whole grains. This doesn't mean "whole grain" bread or cereal, but the actual grains like brown or wild rice, quinoa, barley, amaranth, and millet. Many of these cook in 15-30 minutes in a pot on the stove and stay good in the refrigerator for 5-7 days afterward. This makes it easy to cook once a week and enjoy as leftovers.

The most important dietary change to help constipation is to drink more water. Conveniently, this provides a wide range of other postpartum benefits as well, being helpful for breastfeeding, weight loss, and energy levels, to name a few. But if you want to improve your bowel health, drinking enough water is key. One way the body regulates how hard or soft your stools are is by drawing water from the cells in your intestines into the inside of the intestine, where poop is being formed. In simple terms, this is why increasing fiber—which adds bulk to your stool—without increasing how much water you drink can result in worsening constipation.

Is there anything I can do for my vaginal discomfort, or am I stuck waiting for it to improve?

With the exception of the vaginal bleeding, which generally cannot be altered, there are things you can do to improve all of these things. The hospital staff will usually give you ice packs for your groin, which is the best coping strategy for swelling. Remember that the skin is sensitive, and you will need clothing or a soft cloth between the ice and your skin. Getting up and moving around, although uncomfortable at first, also helps to mobilize fluid out of the skin and back into your circulation.

Stitches usually will dissolve after a couple of weeks. If they irritate you like the mama in the story, check with your doctor to see how soon they can be removed. Healing times can vary widely, and if your body has healed, they will clip your stitches out. Problem solved! Although uncommon, it is possible to be allergic to some types of thread used for stitches. For this reason, severe itching should prompt a visit to your doctor for evaluation.

When should I seek expert help?

For postpartum bleeding/discharge, if you start to have an odor or have pelvic pain or a fever, you need to call your doctor right away. These are possible signs of a post-delivery uterine infection, which can quickly become serious if not treated.

For stitches and swelling, severe pain, and difficulty pooping or peeing are the main signs you should watch for. As noted above, significant itching can be a sign of a stitch allergy. If you received antibiotics during delivery, it can also be a sign of a yeast infection.

For hemorrhoids, you want to watch out for sudden increases in pain or severe itching, which can be signs of inflammation and possibly a blood clot in the hemorrhoid, called a "thrombosed hemorrhoid." The latter can be quite painful and occasionally requires a doctor to open up the hemorrhoid to relieve the pressure.

Thankfully, none of these issues are common. Most of the time, women have minor to moderate discomfort, which resolves over the first couple weeks after the baby is born.

Toolkit

When you leave the hospital, they will often send you home with an assortment of self-care supplies. These include everything from useful items like witch hazel and maxi pads, to the less clearly appealing squirter bottle and the rather dubious one-size-fits-some stretchy mesh disposable panties.

Ice Packs

If you're having swelling, these are key. They are also useful for helping to manage discomfort if you'd rather not take medications. Get a soft, moldable one, (not the hard ones you'd put in a cooler), or simply pick up a bag of frozen peas and label it "not for eating."

Choosing Maxi Pads

If you use pads primarily for your period—and roughly half of women do—this is likely a no-brainer. However, for women who are unaccustomed to wearing pads more than occasionally, this can be a more difficult decision.

Various brands of pads use different materials, deodorizing and bleaching agents, and come in different styles.

Why does this matter? Because you'll be wearing them around the clock for several weeks, increasing the likelihood of skin irritation due to the constant contact of the pad on your skin.

Sometimes irritation is caused by the poor breathability of the pad, by the "wicking" top layer, or by the odor absorbers or other chemicals added to pads by the manufacturer.

Regardless, feeling lousy down there is unpleasant at best—especially since it's on top of all the discomforts from giving birth, like stitches and swelling. Things that can be helpful if you find yourself with irritated skin and need to change brands:

1. Go organic. Removing the chemical bleaches and pesticide residues can make a big difference.
2. Avoid brands with a thin mesh layer on top. The texture can be especially bothersome for some women.
3. Avoid products that are scented.
4. Make sure you change your pad frequently. Sometimes, you can solve the issue simply by using a less absorbent pad and changing it every 2-3 hours.

If all this fails, or if you develop a rash or open sores, call your OB and get evaluated to rule out a skin condition that would require treatment.

Sitz Baths

This is a special kind of bath that you can take to help ease the discomfort in your vaginal area after delivery or for hemorrhoids. The name comes from the German word for sit—"sitzen."

- You can take a sitz bath up to three times a day, for 10-20 minutes each time.

- A sitz bath is different from a regular bath in a couple of key ways:

    1. You're only putting a little water in the bottom of the tub (or using a special basin), so most of you doesn't get wet.
    2. You don't want to use any soap or bubble bath.
    3. You don't want to wash/scrub at all.

Why take a sitz bath? If you just gave birth, the warm water is soothing for your vaginal area. If you have hemorrhoids, they decrease inflammation.

How do you do it?

1. Fill your tub with 3-4 inches of warm water.
2. Add 1/2c Epsom salts if desired. If you have hemorrhoids, you can use 1/4c baking soda instead. (Please don't use both at the same time.)
3. Sit in the water for 10-20 minutes, making sure that the area is submerged; you can add more warm water if needed.
4. If you added Epsom salts or baking soda, rinse off before getting out.
5. Pat yourself dry with a clean towel and dress as usual.

When Giving Birth Involves Surgery

"Let's be clear—a c-section wasn't in my birth plan. I was going to deliver naturally, like I had with my other two babies—no drugs—just me, my husband, and my midwife. I was going to bounce on the birthing ball, sit in the whirlpool, you get the idea. My daughter had other plans. She was stubbornly breech. I was so upset. Sad, angry, all the emotions in one. My OB scheduled me for delivery on my due date, but my water broke almost two weeks before that, so I ended up with the surgeon on call. I think getting out of bed the first couple days was the hardest. I had to push myself around with my arms a lot. And my two-year-old was unhappy because I couldn't pick him up. But the pain, though more than when I'd delivered naturally, was doable. And when HR told me I'd get an extra two weeks of leave, I decided the pain wasn't so bad after all."

—Suzanne, 38, mama of three

What happens in a c-section?

When your baby is born via a c-section instead of vaginally, the symptoms and recovery from birth are obviously different. The issues you have will be influenced by whether or not you were in labor for any length of time before the surgery. Some women go through many hours of labor—and even pushing—without successful vaginal delivery. These women may have some of the issues related to vaginal delivery discussed in the last chapter, in addition to c-section specific issues.

In a c-section, your doctor will cut an opening across your abdomen and then make a similar cut across your uterus to deliver your baby. In non-emergency situations, these cuts are usually made across your lower abdomen from side to side, near the bikini line. This is to promote the strongest healing of your uterus, muscles, and skin. The location also minimizes the cosmetic effects of the procedure. Let me clarify—you certainly will have a scar. But your doctor will do everything in his/her power to minimize it without compromising the safety of you or your baby. The differences in recovery from a c-section versus a vaginal delivery exist primarily because it is a major surgery. Your overall recovery will be longer, and there are a few differences related to the surgery itself.

What is the usual recovery from a c-section?

Most women who have a typical c-section delivery will recover from the surgery in about six weeks. Some women will feel nearly normal in about four weeks. For others, it may take several months. It depends on individual factors related to your body prior to the surgery such as your baseline level of health and fitness, body weight, and your nutritional level.

In the first week, most women experience some degree of pain and swelling, both in the abdominal wall and in the uterus. This will be primarily around where the surgeon made the cut to deliver your baby. You will have medications available to you, both prescription and over the counter, as directed by your doctor to help with this. You will find that certain positions and movements will help your pain, and others will make it worse. In this fragile early stage, most doctors recommend limiting your activity level. You should mostly rest and walk around your home and not lift anything heavier than your newborn baby.

After a week or two, you'll be given the okay to walk around more. Most women are still sore and tender, but you should notice some improvement. One month after surgery, you've usually been cleared to resume driving (assuming you are off pain medications), and you can start taking longer walks. By six weeks, when you are seen for your check-up, your wounds should be mostly healed. Unless there were complications, most women are cleared to resume regular activity at this time.

What symptoms are common after a c-section?

Like a vaginal delivery, you will have vaginal bleeding and discharge as your uterus sheds the extra lining that helps support your baby's growth. Your uterus will still be enlarged right after delivery, and it will take several weeks to shrink to its normal size.

You can expect to have some pain around where your surgical incision is. In cutting through skin and dividing muscles, your doctor will inevitably cut through tiny nerve endings to the skin.

This is unavoidable and is one part of why you have pain, but it can also cause small areas of numbness. How much you notice this varies widely. Some women don't notice anything, while others have large patches of numbness or burning sensations around part of their incision. Everyone is different. Both the superficial pain and the numbness gradually improve with time as the nerves heal.

What should I watch for after a c-section?

The most common problem women can develop after a surgical delivery is an infection in the skin around the incision. This shows up as increased redness, pain, and swelling around the incision. You may have fluid draining from part of your wound. If you see any of these things, contact your doctor right away.

You can also get an infection in the uterus itself—either in the area of the incision or in the overall lining of the uterus. This is something that can happen regardless of how you deliver, but it's 10 to 30 times more common if you've had a c-section. The most common symptoms of this type of infection are fever, increase in pain over your uterus, and change in vaginal bleeding/discharge (looks different, smells bad). This type of infection can get worse quickly. If you start having these symptoms, make sure you call your doctor immediately. [1]

Most women worry about their incision staying together. Although the likelihood of it splitting wide open is rare, it is less uncommon for a small area to open up. When this happens, it often drains a small amount of clear yellowish fluid. The wound is more likely to open up if you are having symptoms of a wound infection. In this situation, your doctor may remove a stitch or two to allow any pus or fluid to drain out. In most cases, you will have to wear an extra bandage over the wound, and it will take a few extra weeks to heal fully, but other major problems are unlikely.

Your wound is also more likely to open up if you are significantly overweight at the time of delivery, or if you have a condition or take a medication that affects your body's ability to heal normally. In these situations, your doctor may recommend that you wear an abdominal binder for a longer period of time. They may also choose to reinforce your wound with a special type of stitches or wound dressings to provide the skin with extra support.

Because a c-section is a major surgery, it also increases your risk for blood clots. This risk is already increased because of the hormones of pregnancy, but having major surgery increases it a little bit further. So, if you get leg swelling, especially just in one leg, or suddenly find yourself short of breath or having chest pain, you should be urgently checked out in the ER.

Everyone worries about major surgical complications like internal bleeding and having the stitches fall apart, however these issues are uncommon. Prolonged and excessive bleeding can happen but is more commonly related to pregnancy-specific factors like how the placenta was attached or the uterus itself. Statistically speaking, although a c-section is a major surgery, most women do fine. At the end of the day, the most important thing is to contact your doctor if you don't feel right. Getting evaluated sooner rather than later can make a big difference. [2]

What can I do to help my body heal after a c-section?

The most important thing to do is follow your doctor's instructions about what kinds of activity and lifting you can and cannot do. The restrictions are there for a reason. Your body is very weak at your incisions, and it's hard for your body to heal properly if you're constantly doing things that put the stitches under a lot of tension. Most doctors will say not to lift anything heavier than your newborn baby, and there are usually limits on things like walking, climbing, and driving.

From a nutritional perspective, ensuring you are getting plenty of fresh, whole, healthy foods and continuing to take your prenatal vitamins are also important. In pregnancy and breastfeeding, your body often runs low on many nutrients because it uses what you take in to support the growth—and the feeding—of your baby. To maximize healing, it is especially important to get enough of all three major calorie categories—protein, fat, and carbohydrates. Vitamins, especially Vitamin C, and minerals such as zinc, are key to good wound healing. This is why taking your vitamins and eating lots of fruits and vegetables plays an underappreciated role in healing.

Early on, using an abdominal binder, which is often given to you at the hospital, can support your abdominal wall and decrease the strain placed on your skin, soft tissue, and muscles. Wearing your binder also helps with pain around the incision. Binder use is especially important when you are up and about for the first 2-4 weeks after surgery or if you are significantly overweight. Extra weight, especially around your middle, increases the stress on your incision line. This can slow healing speed and increase your risk of having part of the incision reopen.

Toolkit

Wound Healing Stir-Fry

Vitamin C and Zinc are two key nutrients for wound healing, and this recipe packs a healthy punch of both, with vitamin C from the bell pepper and broccoli, and tons of zinc from the beef, pinto beans, and cashews. If you purchase pre-sliced beef and a bag of chopped broccoli, the prep is minimal. And if you don't have a spice shelf in your kitchen, feel free to try your favorite pre-packaged fajita seasoning mix instead of making your own.

- 1 large red bell pepper, sliced in bite-sized pieces
- 2 cups broccoli, also in bite sized pieces
- ¼ cup diced onion
- ¾ pound beef sirloin or strip steak, cut in thin slices
- 1 cup canned pinto beans, rinsed well
- ¼ cup cashews, chopped

Seasoning mix: 1 tsp smoked paprika, 1/2 tsp oregano, 1/2 tsp chili powder, 1/8 tsp chipotle pepper (okay to substitute cayenne pepper), 1 tsp salt, dash of pepper

Heat a nonstick skillet over medium heat and add the beef, onion, and half of the seasoning mix and sauté until onion is translucent and meat is browned. Remove to a plate or bowl. Into the same pan, add 1 tbsp of oil and the bell peppers, cook 2-3 minutes before adding the broccoli and sprinkle with seasoning mix (start with about half of the remaining mix and add extra to taste). Stir frequently until veggies reach desired level of tenderness. Then add back the beef and onion, as well as the canned pinto beans and mix well to blend. Serve over brown rice and sprinkle with chopped cashews. If you have a nut allergy, try chunks of avocado or a dollop of guacamole.

Taking Care of Your Abdominal Binder

- For a variety of reasons, most abdominal binders are white. And being made mostly of elastic materials, they don't breathe very well, which means that many women find them useful—but hot and sweaty.
- If you are wearing your binder as recommended, there is a good likelihood that sooner or later, you will want to wash it.
- The safest way to clean your binder is to wash it out in the sink by hand using a mild detergent like Dreft or Woolite, though many women use their regular laundry soap.
- Fill the sink or a small basin with cold water and add a little bit of soap. If you have a stain on the binder, scrub that first. Then, let the binder soak in the water for 10-20 minutes. Follow this by a good rinse in clean water.
- Hang your binder to dry over a rack or your shower curtain rod. Do not wear it again until fully dried.

Diastasis Recti

"As a 'new mom' gift, a friend of mine bought me a package at a local yoga studio I'd always talked about trying but never gotten around to. After my doctor cleared me for exercise, I signed up for my first class. I managed to stuff my breasts into an old sports bra and was super excited when my pre-baby leggings fit. But everything went downhill from there. It was SO HARD. I was wobbling and falling all over the place; I couldn't hold any of the positions for more than a few seconds. The instructor came over to correct my form, and I fell over backwards. Cue the exhausted, emotional new mom waterworks. As she's helping me sit up, tears running down my cheeks, she looks at my stomach and says, 'Oh, you have diastasis.' I was like, huh? She told me what it was and that it wasn't my fault I couldn't do the poses. I did finish the class. I'm proud of myself for that because I really, really wanted to give up and go home. When I went back after three months of physical therapy, I found her and thanked her, and she said that once upon a time, she'd had diastasis, too."

—Lisa, 31, mama of one

What is diastasis recti?

Diastasis recti (DIE-uh-STAY-sis wreck-TIE) is a Latin medical term that means separation of the abdominal muscles. Diastasis means a separation between two parts. Recti refers to the rectus abdominis—the big ab muscle that covers your belly. You know, the one that gives you a six-pack. Except right after you have a baby, there's no six-pack. And here's why.

When you are pregnant, you are growing a tiny human who takes up progressively more space. This stretches out your abdominal muscles, particularly the rectus abdominis, which covers the front of your abdomen. Often, the muscle fibers will take the path of less resistance, and instead of continuing to stretch and possibly tear, they will start to separate in the middle, sliding to either side of your growing belly. The thin band of connective tissue in the middle—called the linea alba—then stretches and expands. Remember when we talked about stretch marks and connective tissue stretching in the skin chapter? This is the same idea. The flatter your pre-baby belly and the more "stuck on basketball" look you had during pregnancy, the more stretching is required.

After your baby is born, the muscles don't immediately return to their original length and location. Like the collagen and elastin we talked about in Santa Claus belly, muscle fibers have their length and shape because of chemical bonds between them. These bonds adjusted themselves to a size that would accommodate your pregnant body. Now, they must break and re-form multiple times to gradually pull your ab muscles back into their original shape. The linea alba also has to contract back into a thin line. Though it is fairly elastic, sometimes this process takes extra time or doesn't fully work the way it should.

How common is diastasis recti, and why does it happen?

Immediately after delivery, most women have some degree of diastasis. By six weeks after delivery, this number has dropped to around 50%. At one year, however, about 30% percent of women still have measurable diastasis according to the *British Journal of Sports Medicine*.

In some women, the muscles and connective tissue remain somewhat stretched out. There's no clear consensus in the medical community on what increases your risk for diastasis recti. Originally, we thought that older age at pregnancy, baby size, number of babies, body weight, diabetes, and c-sections could all possibly be linked to it. Medical research over the last five to ten years, however, has not found any clear association for any of these. That said, having multiple potential risk factors probably does increase your odds. And from a physiological standpoint, things like flat pre-pregnancy abs, big baby carried way out in front, high flexibility, and age—because when we get older, our tissues get looser to decreased collagen—are likely to contribute on some level.[1, 4]

How do I know how bad my diastasis is?

In medicine, we measure diastasis by how many fingertips fit into the space between the ab muscles. Your doctor can measure this at your postpartum visit, but it's fairly easy to check yourself at home if you are curious. Please do not do this test if you are less than eight weeks post c-section or if your doctor has given you any ongoing activity restrictions. Just lie on your back, then lift your head and shoulders off the bed. You will see a v-shaped mountain running down your belly if you have any diastasis. Poke it down with a fingertip and feel for the firm sides of the ab muscles. Then, hold your fingers like you're wearing a mitten and see how many fingertips you can squeeze in between the two sides of your ab muscles. There are various systems for labeling how severe the separation is and where it should be measured, but in general, anything less than two fingers is considered normal, less than three is mild, three to five is considered moderate, and greater than five is severe.

What can I do to fix my diastasis recti?

That was the first question I asked my OB when I realized that I had a whopping 4-5 finger split in my previously flat stomach after the birth of my eight-pound son. The answer surprised me because it wasn't doing traditional abdominal exercises like crunches and planks. In fact, these are some of the worst exercises you can do, particularly early on in your postpartum course. Exercises like these increase the pressure inside your abdomen. They don't help and can even worsen diastasis and weak pelvic floor muscle problems (we'll talk about these in the next two chapters). What is helpful is starting gradually with isometric exercises that have you tighten the ab muscles without actually moving your body. Kegels are the best-known isometric exercise for your pelvic muscles. Which exercises you do and how many are determined by how long it's been since you had your baby, the type of birth (vaginal or c-section), how severe your ab split is, and other factors. In the toolkit at the end of this chapter, I've put together a few of the best starter exercises and other resources to help you on the road to healing. [2,3]

When should I seek medical care for diastasis recti?

The short answer is always. First, you want to have the diagnosis and severity determined by a medical professional. You also need to ensure you don't have an umbilical hernia to go with it. You should be checked for pelvic floor problems that can be seen alongside diastasis as well. These can be evaluated by your OB or primary care doctor at a regular office visit.

If you have diastasis, you can get a referral for some combination of regular physical therapy, pelvic floor physical therapy, or pilates-based physical therapy. You will have an initial evaluation, followed by a certain number of visits once or twice a week for a half hour each. You will do supervised exercises and be given exercises to do at home. How successful therapy is will depend in large part on doing those home exercises consistently and continuing them even after your allotted number of visits are up. Insurance usually allows between 4 and 12 sessions, but full recovery can take months.[2,3]

If this was my first baby and I plan to get pregnant again, is it worth it to try to improve/cure my diastasis?

Absolutely! It will likely happen again, but by getting your ab muscles and linea alba as close to normal position as possible, you'll be decreasing the severity of further episodes and increasing the odds of a better final result after you're done having kids.

I had my last baby five years ago. Is it too late to try to fix my diastasis?

Nope! It's never too late. Women have improved or even closed their ab separation five, even ten years or more after last giving birth. It will require effort. Just like going to the gym and lifting weights to strengthen your arms, your ab muscles require time and consistent effort to get stronger. But improvement, and even recovery, is certainly possible.

What about surgery? Can't they tie my abs back together?

Yes… and no. As someone who has had a long struggle with diastasis, I can tell you that surgery is not as easy of a fix as it sounds. Surgery for diastasis recti without a hernia is usually performed as part of a procedure known as abdominoplasty—a.k.a a "tummy tuck." Unfortunately, that means it won't be covered by insurance. The good news is that the likelihood that the problem will reoccur in the hands of a good surgeon is close to zero. So, if you choose to invest in the procedure, it is usually effective. But it is an investment and does carry risks.

If you have a hernia associated with your diastasis, you may be able to have at least a partial repair of your diastasis as part of hernia surgery. But this is something to discuss with your surgeon at your consultation, as it may or may not be possible.[3]

> *"I had a tummy tuck. It's not something I advertise because I feel like people will judge me as vain and superficial. But I don't lie about it either. At 5'2 tall, I'm pretty petite, and I've never been overweight. But we had to do Clomid to get pregnant, and I ended up having twins. On top of it all, I had a lower abdominal tattoo from my college days. You should've seen what it looked like when I finally delivered. Afterward, it didn't seem to matter how hard I worked; when I sat up, it looked like a mountain range had formed down the middle of my stomach. Then I started having back pain. And to add insult to injury, my tattoo looked as absurd as it had when I was pregnant. So, I did it. I had so much extra skin that the doctor could cut off my tattoo entirely. No regrets. It's not for everyone, but it worked out great for me."*
>
> **(Tammy, 28, mother of twin girls.)**

The Hidden Cost of Diastasis—My Story

Diastasis recti was one of the key issues driving the idea for this book. Why? Because I have it, and this part of the book is deeply personal because I've been there. I've looked at my own body, felt my own body. I did the research; I tried the things. Lots of them, in fact. And I shed more than a few tears along the way. And three years after my last baby, I still refuse to believe that my story has reached the end.

In 2017, when I got pregnant for the first time, I was certainly "old" by medical standards, but I was healthy and fit. As a holistic physician, I practiced what I preached and reaped the benefits. I ran, was a competitive adult figure skater, and I played multiple sports. The day before I found out I was pregnant, I biked 30 miles with a good friend on an annual community ride.

I had one of those basketball pregnancies, you know, the kind where you're all belly from the front and normal appearing from the back. My belly button disappeared completely early on, and I still don't know how I managed to avoid stretch marks.

After I delivered my son, nearly eight pounds and over 21 inches long despite being three weeks early, I couldn't wait for my OB to release me to start skating and exercising again. Except I couldn't even get in and out of bed without climbing on the platform base. My belly button still looked all stretched and weird. I struggled with back and abdominal pain when taking my newborn son on walks around the lake near our home. Then, one morning as I was trying to sit up in bed, I realized that my stomach did something weird.

As a Family Medicine physician, I trained in obstetrics and knew what diastasis was. Still, I hadn't encountered it much in clinical practice. When I checked myself, I discovered I had more than a four-finger split, and literally couldn't sit up without using my arms to push myself. I cried in frustration more days than not as my body repeatedly failed me.

I did my research. I found a good ebook with an exercise plan. I thought for sure with time and effort, it would go away. I did physical therapy, pelvic physical therapy, and pilates with an instructor who was a fellow adult skater. After a year, the split was down to about a finger, which most guidelines consider normal.

Does anybody else feel the irony here? How is something obviously not normal in a woman's body labeled normal?

My improvement became a moot point because I got pregnant again. Except this time, I delivered during the middle of the pandemic, and those therapy options were not available. With a toddler, a newborn, and a medical career during COVID, I was honestly too stressed out and exhausted to care. Or that's what I told myself.

The Physical Costs of Diastasis

What I didn't realize early on was the physical toll diastasis took on the rest of my body. I had this aching mild abdominal pain sometimes in the afternoon and evenings. I had a lot of lower back and hip pain. And carrying around my newborn baby, even in a swaddle, was ridiculously difficult. According to the Cleveland Clinic, in addition to my issues, diastasis also can cause pain with intercourse, urine leakage, and constipation.[4]

Insurance companies label diastasis as a cosmetic problem. I disagree. True disability aside, there are few things that are as physically challenging in day-to-day life as having severely weakened core muscles. Your abdominal muscles are the key stabilizers for your body for upright movement. Every time you sit on the sofa and lean sideways to reach for something or lean over the crib to pick up your baby or do basic daily activities like emptying the dishwasher, you're using your abdominal muscles.

Weak abdominal muscles lead to increased reliance on your back muscles to stabilize your torso. This often causes back pain and posture changes and can set you up for a host of problems down the road.

This is why doing the exercises and safely strengthening your ab muscles is so important. Even if your diastasis never entirely goes away, strengthening your abs and learning how to safely brace and protect them can make a huge difference in your quality of life for years to come.

The Emotional Costs of Diastasis Recti

As women, we're inundated with social media images of what our bodies should look like. None of those images involve a mom pooch or an abdominal wall resembling a mountain range. There's nothing fun or sexy about looking like you're five months pregnant two years after having a baby. And there's something very defeating about finally losing all the baby weight, only to discover you still have a muffin top that wasn't there before.

If you're struggling with emotions surrounding diastasis and your new post-delivery body, you're not alone. It's common to feel upset, frustrated, and embarrassed. Medical research shows that having diastasis is associated with lower body self-esteem and that lack of a good social support system compounds the issue. Is it right that society makes us feel this way? Of course not, but that doesn't make what we're going through less important.

For now, I will simply say "hey, I've been there, and I get it." I was an athlete before becoming a mama and I learned the hard way that much of my self-worth was tied to being strong and fit. I've battled through tears of frustration, shame, and self-loathing over the fact that my body no longer looks and behaves like it used to. I've come out emotionally stronger for it—but believe me, I still have some extra belly to work with. Now, I'm here to help you find grace for yourself and love for the body that was strong enough to grow and birth a little one for you to love. You've got this, mama.

Toolkit

The number one key to healing your abs is to learn to brace your abdominal muscles effectively. This prevents strain and injury from both exercise and daily activity. To perform a brace, you want to basically suck in your stomach like you are trying to be as thin as possible, focusing on drawing everything in around your belly button. Then, hold the muscles firm and tight like you are preparing to defend yourself against a punch to the stomach. Practice this at least three times a day, holding for 15-30 seconds each time.

When to use the abdominal brace:
- When lifting something up
- When getting up out of bed
- When you cough/sneeze or blow your nose
- For any activity that takes you away from your center of gravity

Other basic exercises that can help you begin the healing process:

Overhead reaches: lie on your back, knees bent, arms extended overhead on the ground above you. Move your arms in an arc through the air until they are lying flat at your side, then return through the same arc back over your head. Make sure you brace your abs and press your lower back into the floor during this exercise.

Toe touches: lie on your back, knees bent to 90 degrees, shins parallel with the floor. Brace your abs and press your lower back to the ground. Then, slowly lower the toes of one leg to the ground and raise back up to the original position. Repeat on the other side. Do a set of 6-10 on each leg.

Bridge: lie on your back, knees bent to 90 degrees. Tighten your pelvic muscles like you are doing a kegel, then brace your abs, press your lower back to the floor, and slowly roll your butt and low back off the ground until you reach a bridge position. Hold for 3-5 seconds, then slowly lower. Repeat 4-6 times.

Modified side plank: lie on your side, bottom leg bent at the knee. Brace your abs. Raise up onto the elbow of your bottom arm, with the elbow positioned in a line underneath your shoulder. Your weight should be balanced between your elbow, your knee, and the foot of the top leg. Hold the position for 15-20 seconds, trying to draw your abs in like a belt around your waist.

Sit to stand: sit in a kitchen chair, shoulders down, abs drawn in, hips tucked beneath you. Stand up slowly like you are getting up from a squat, without using your hands to help, if possible. Then lower yourself back down to the chair like you are doing a squat—abs still braced, pelvis tucked—tightening your butt muscles. Repeat 6-10 times.

Yikes, I Just Wet My Pants

"This is kind of embarrassing, but I was running errands one morning with my kids about three months after my youngest was born. I'd gotten groceries, went to Sam's Club for diapers, all the things. By the time we headed home, I had to pee. It wasn't so bad when we were leaving the store, but by the time I was halfway home, I was dancing around in the driver's seat, praying for green lights. Then we turned, and the sun came out from behind a cloud, hitting me full force in the face. I've got pretty sensitive eyes. So I sneezed. And as that sneeze came out, a bunch of urine came out, too. Not like a few drops. Like a giant gush. Thank goodness the car had leather seats. When I got home, I pulled into the garage, left the kids strapped into their seats, and literally sprinted to the bathroom, dribbling and dripping the whole way. My three-year-old thought it was a hoot. Me? Let's just say I've gotten over my issues with public restrooms."

—**Amanda, 34, mama of two**

Why does having a baby cause all these problems down there?!

Inside your pelvis sits your uterus, ovaries, bladder, and the bottom part of your large intestine on its way out of the body. All of these organs sit atop a dome-shaped sheet of muscle called the pelvic floor. Additionally, they are all held in place by different ligaments. For example, two main ligaments hold the bladder in place—one fastens it to the pubic bone in front, and the other to the inside of your belly button up high.

When you are pregnant, the ligaments attached to your uterus are under a lot of strain trying to hold up your growing baby. You may have heard about "round ligament pain" in your second and early third trimester. This is why that pain can develop. But the pelvic floor muscle also gets a major workout as it has to support your growing uterus (baby) anytime you're upright.

The pelvic floor muscle is one of the key players in controlling urination. When combined with the pressure on your bladder from your baby, this is why many women leak urine late in pregnancy. We all expect it to go away once the baby is born, but sometimes it doesn't.

Why am I leaking urine?

Because the pelvic floor is often stretched and strained during pregnancy and delivery, it doesn't always function normally once the baby is born. Although I talk about it as one muscle, it's several small muscles that all share some common attachments and layer together to form that single sheet we call the pelvic floor. Some of these muscles are specifically tasked with controlling the flow of urine out of the body from the bladder. When these muscles are overstretched, they don't hold their default tight "contracted" shape the way they used to. This makes it easier for urine to leave the bladder and the body, especially when under pressure.

Things like having a full bladder, having someone push on your lower abdomen, and coughing/sneezing/jumping all increase the force pushing urine out of the bladder. In other words, all these things make those muscles work harder to keep you from urinating unintentionally. Before you had kids, when those muscles were healthy and strong, they functioned normally, and you never gave things a second thought. After being stretched and overworked for months holding up a baby, then working at maximal force to push out a baby, they don't always function the way they used to.

In other words, sometimes, the force coming from the bladder is greater than the strength of the muscles holding the urine up. When this happens, a little bit (or a not-so-little bit) of urine escapes, and you are mortified to realize that you just urinated in your underwear.

How do I make this stop fast?

Unfortunately, there is no quick fix to urinary incontinence (the fancy medical term for leaking urine). But you can do a few things to help yourself almost immediately. First, get into the habit of using the restroom every few hours. A mostly empty bladder is much less likely to leak urine than a full one. Second, avoid bladder irritants. These are foods/beverages that can irritate the lining of the bladder and make it more likely that you will lose control of your urine. The most common ones are alcohol and caffeine, but tea and coffee, carbonated beverages, chocolate, and artificial sweeteners also make the list. As does smoking.

Are there any real solutions?

Yes. The first one is to start doing your kegels. And not just the random kegels when you're sitting around, but focused sets of kegels two or three times a day. To get an idea of how they should feel to be effective, once you start peeing, try to stop the flow of urine a couple of times as you're going.

Next, get conscious of your body alignment. After having a baby, most women continue to have a belly forward and butt backward posture with an exaggerated arch in the back. Standing and swaying with a newborn doesn't help this. What you want to do is to suck your belly in, flatten out your lower back, and tilt your pelvis under. That helps align the muscles and ligaments in the pelvic floor better to function properly.

Third, talk to your doctor and go to physical therapy. Yes, they have physical therapy for this. There are specialized therapists who only work with the pelvis. Some of the exercises will be for your abs, back, and hips. Other exercises will be specifically designed to work some of those pelvic floor muscles. This type of physical therapy often involves some type of exam of the vaginal muscles, which can feel a little awkward.

"I was so embarrassed to go to my first pelvic therapy appointment! I showed up at the last minute with a baseball hat and a giant sweatshirt—as if I could somehow hide. When she explained what she was going to do, my face went bright red, and I just wanted to disappear. It helped a lot, though, and I'm glad I did it. Thankfully, after the first time, it was a lot less weird. I just hope I never run into her at Target!" (Alexa, 29, mama of twins.)

There is nothing glamorous about having someone feel your muscles as you tighten them through your vagina. But every pelvic floor physical therapist I know is wonderfully kind and sympathetic and explains what will happen. And they're almost universally women, as well. In most cases, if you do your daily exercises and continue to do them for several months, you will have good improvement.[1]

What about medications or surgery? Can someone just go in and fix it?

Surgery is usually not a great option, though if you have surgery for other pelvic floor issues, you may see benefits to your urine leakage, too. The reason it's of limited benefit is that you don't really want to permanently fix the opening for urine tighter, as that can give you difficulty urinating at all.

There are several prescription medications for urinary incontinence. A lot of them are more focused on the "gotta go, gotta go" issue than the "I cough and I pee" issue, but many women do have components of both. Your doctor may suggest a trial of medication, where you take a new prescription daily for a few weeks or a month, and then see if it makes any difference. If it does, then you can continue the medication. If not, there is no sense in spending your money on it.

I just had my first baby, and I am leaking urine. Will it get worse if I have more babies?

Maybe. First, I'd encourage you to go through therapy before getting pregnant again. Getting things as good as they can be (or all the way better) will help improve your odds of having fewer problems with your next baby. Some women have problems with each successive pregnancy, but others do not. Remember that each pregnancy is different and that so many things go into your overall health during the pregnancy and can impact the results.

Toolkit

Kegels

Ah, kegels, the most widely known exercise for women's health. Why? Because they're straightforward to perform, require no special equipment, and can be done anywhere.

After delivery, when your pelvic floor is weaker, start doing them lying down. As you get stronger, you can progress to sitting and then standing positions.

The goal is to tighten the muscles of your vagina without tightening up the whole rest of your body (legs, abs, back).

It is okay to stop the flow of urine once or twice if you are having trouble isolating these muscles, but this isn't something you should continue to do. Ironically, it often makes urine leakage worse in the long term—and worse is not what we're going for by doing the extra work.

There are a couple of different ways to perform kegels. One is to squeeze and hold the contraction for 15-20 seconds before releasing and repeating. The other is to squeeze and then release rapidly and repeatedly. I recommend you do them both multiple times per day, doing a set of them until the muscles feel weak and tired, then taking a short break and repeating.

Most of the time, you will need to give your body two or three months before deciding whether or not something is helping you. Although, some women do see changes much faster, usually eight weeks is about the window for seeing measurable change. I always encourage women to keep a log to know when and how often symptoms recur. Otherwise, there's just no basis for comparison.

Pad Choice

Depending on how often you leak and how much, you may find yourself wearing some protection on a daily or nearly daily basis. This can increase the risk of irritating the sensitive skin in this area.

Options for managing leakage include using regular pantyliners and maxipads, but also pads or special underwear made specifically for this use. The big brands for these products are Poise and Depends. Although, shopping for these products might feel very embarrassing, they are worth considering.

Pads designed for your period are made to absorb blood, which is thicker than urine and comes out more slowly. Pads designed for incontinence are made to absorb urine, which is thinner and comes out quickly in bursts. If you leak more than a few drops at a time, you will typically have better results with a product made for incontinence. Products labeled for incontinence also have chemicals that help neutralize the distinctive smell of urine.

Avoiding Bladder Irritants

In addition to doing therapy to help rebuild the pelvic floor muscles, specific foods can make your bladder more irritable—or "twitchy" as I like to think of it. These foods and beverages increase the likelihood that you will leak urine in the exposure of a given trigger. Which items affect you will be somewhat individual, as will the degree of impact.

The list includes caffeine and alcohol (these are probably not a surprise), carbonation, artificial sweeteners, and acidic foods like citrus fruits and tomatoes. More than a few of my patients drank several bottles of no-calorie, fizzy, flavored water daily to stay hydrated while nursing, only to find that their bladder symptoms improved measurably when they switched to plain tap water with fresh fruit.

It's All Falling Out

"When my son was born, I had a lot of swelling down there. He had to be induced. They said that was super weird for a fourth baby, but he was happy in there. And he ended up being huge, which I'm sure didn't help; I mean, I'm not exactly a big person. It took so long for the swelling to go away that I got used to feeling weird down there. Until one day, I picked up my four-year-old (not a great idea, but she was sick and crying) and literally felt something coming out of my vagina. OMG it was so bizarre. I almost dropped her to run to the bathroom before whatever "it" was ended up in my underwear instead of in the toilet. Except that "it" ended up being attached to me. I called my OB having a panic attack; the nurse was so nice, they worked me in that afternoon, and I started treatment the next week."

—Lisa, 36, mama of four

What exactly is pelvic organ prolapse?

Basically, it's when one or more of your pelvic organs—your uterus, bladder, rectum—"falls" from its usual location to take up space in the vaginal canal and even sometimes to fully protrude from the body through the vaginal opening.

The first time you realize you have prolapse, it can be scary. Sometimes, you feel the sensation that something is there, like a tampon that isn't quite all the way in. You reach down with your fingers or look with a mirror and find a bulge of tissue that wasn't there before. It usually isn't painful; it's just there.

In more severe cases, you might suddenly see or feel something protruding from your vagina. Most women have the sudden anxiety of "Oh my gosh, what is this thing?" If you try to push it back in, sometimes it works, and sometimes it gradually slides its way back out. You may be terrified of having a tumor or part of your placenta still inside you.

All of these thoughts are normal. To be honest, freaking out is normal, too. After all, if you don't work in gynecology, you've probably never heard of prolapse. It's not exactly the headline topic in magazines or social media. So, I'm here to remind you to take a deep breath and keep reading. We'll talk about why prolapse happens and what you can do about it—because suffering in silence doesn't make for a good quality of life. Many women are too embarrassed to talk about it.

Why does prolapse happen?

Back in the chapters on diastasis and urinary incontinence, we talked about how some ligaments and muscles hold up the contents of your pelvis, namely the uterus, ovaries, and bladder. Your colon (large intestine) also passes through here on its way to becoming your rectum and exiting your body. We're going to dive into this a bit deeper so you can better understand what's going on and how different treatments can affect your symptoms.

Your uterus and bladder each have a couple of ligaments holding them in place. They also both sit on top of the pelvic floor muscles. You remember that the pelvic floor is a series of interconnected muscles that work together to form a giant sheet of muscle holding everything up. When you are pregnant, these muscles and ligaments work together to keep things in their (relatively) proper place. However, that extra workload for weeks and months on end places them under a lot of strain, and they can get stretched out and even develop microscopic tears. This causes them not to bounce back immediately after the baby is born when they are no longer working so hard. It takes time for the muscle fibers to shorten up, and 3-6 weeks for the microscopic tears to heal—just like with a muscle strain anywhere else in the body.

The muscles of the pelvic floor also undergo acute stress during a vaginal delivery. But it's not because they're the muscles doing the pushing. It's primarily your abdominal muscles—specifically the transverse abdominis—that push the baby out of your body. This is the deepest of all your ab muscles and forms a corset around your core from ribs to pelvis. For your baby to be born, this muscle sheet tightens. But your pelvic floor has to relax. That's right, for your baby to be born, your pelvic floor must relax and stretch out. If you are tense and tight or have a very large baby, these muscles are more stressed and more likely to tear. In an article for the Department of Health and Human Services[1] in the UK, they cite multiple contributory factors, include duration of labor, complex tears during delivery, number of pregnancies, and needing an operative vaginal delivery—where your doctor uses special instruments to help bring the baby through the last little bit of the birth canal and out of your body. Non-obstetrical risk factors include older age and obesity.

All of these things increase the risk of damage to an essential group of muscles called the levator ani. These muscles are instrumental in holding your organs in their proper places and in controlling urine. When they are damaged a little bit, they cannot hold their tight position when under stress. What places them under stress? Anything that increases the pressure from above—coughing/sneezing, jumping up and down (gravity), bearing down, and most traditional abdominal exercises like sit-ups. When the levator ani is damaged a lot, it is unable to function properly even without stress, and one or more organs can start to sag down into the vagina. If this sag is mild, you might not even notice until you go to put a tampon in, and things feel different. But if the sag is severe, you can have the sensation something is there or even see something protruding from your vagina.

This sight is quite unsettling for most women. The sensations can range from painless fullness, like with a poorly placed tampon, to moderate levels of pain. Severe pain is uncommon with prolapse and should always trigger an evaluation for other conditions. Possible prolapse warrants a phone call to your doctor as soon as it's noticed for a formal evaluation.

Can prolapse happen even years after delivery?

YES! There are two reasons why this can happen. The first is that pelvic floor damage is a cumulative process. If the muscles are not re-trained and used properly, the symptoms can occur or progress with time. This is particularly true if you gain a large amount of weight, as this alone will increase the pressure on the pelvic floor.

The second reason is changing hormone levels. As you near menopause and estrogen levels start to fall, this leads to a decrease in the strength of the tissue surrounding the vagina and pelvic floor, which can lead to new or worsening prolapse.

Why do I have trouble pooping with prolapse?

Rectal prolapse is a special kind of prolapse that affects your ability to poop. As stool exits your body through the rectum, it passes directly underneath the vagina. Think of holding two empty toilet paper rolls to make binoculars, then turn them so they are stacked, one atop the other. The two tunnels share a common wall, which is usually not very stretchy. But when you have a baby vaginally, that common wall is under a lot of pressure as you try to push the baby's head out. This can cause damage to that common wall, even if you don't have an outright tear.

A damaged wall will be unable to keep stool in the small space in the small intestinal tube, and the intestines will bulge upwards into the vaginal area when filled with stool or when you are trying to have a bowel movement. If you tend towards constipation or very formed bowel movements, this will make it harder to push poop out of your body. In severe cases, you may have to place your thumb or fingers into your vagina and push down on the bulge to be able to poop easier. If you had a lot of tearing during delivery, this should be discussed with your doctor right away, as nerve damage can also be an issue.

For most women, however, rectal prolapse is not a severe issue and can be easily managed by developing good bowel habits and using a stool softener when needed. Constipation can usually be managed with a few simple health habits. These include drinking plenty of water, eating plenty of fresh fruits and vegetables (your goal is 25-30g of fiber), and moving your body daily through low-impact activity.

What can I do about my prolapse?

The first line of treatment for prolapse is pelvic physical therapy. As discussed in chapter six, this is a particular physical therapy targeting your pelvic floor muscles. The goal is to strengthen and balance these muscles so they can do their job more effectively.

However, the real key to therapy lies in what you do between formal sessions. When you go to your therapy sessions, the therapist will also give you exercises to perform daily at home. Your ability to put in the daily work at home (usually at most 10-20 minutes) will play a key role in determining what kind of recovery you have.

What if therapy doesn't work?

Sometimes, no matter how hard you work and how much you try, your prolapse just doesn't get better. For women with mild disease, that is often not a major problem. They attend low-impact instead of high-impact aerobics classes, empty their bladder regularly, and often don't have any issues that impact their quality of life. For women with isolated issues with their uterus, being fitted with a device called a pessary is one possibility. This is a small doughnut-shaped silicone or plastic device. It fits into your vaginal area and can be inserted and removed like a tampon. For women with severe prolapse, however, the thought of going through life with constant bladder leakage, bowel problems, or having to poke their uterus up every time they cough or sneeze is profoundly life-impacting. In these situations, surgical treatment to tack things into place is worth considering.

Toolkit

Pelvic Floor Exercises

Although I strongly recommend pursuing formal pelvic physical therapy if you have access to it, there are a few simple exercises that any woman can start with to help improve pelvic floor strength. As noted previously, you won't see improvement overnight, so it's important to be consistent for at least 6-8 weeks. Remember, there will also be some overlap; exercises that help prolapse will often help with bladder leakage and diastasis, as well.

The first step is kegels. Please review the information in the toolkit from the previous chapter. There are a few different ways you can do kegels. The traditional way is to tighten the muscles and hold for at least ten seconds, then release. However, doing a much quicker kegel, where you tighten and relax the muscles at 1-2 second intervals, also has value. When you start out, do a couple of sets of 10-20 kegels twice a day, then increase a little bit every few days as your muscles get stronger.

The next exercise is a bridge or hip raise. Lay on your back with your knees bent and feet flat on the floor. Tighten your pelvic floor muscles (aka do a kegel and hold) and then slowly lift your hips off the floor until your butt and low back are raised as high as you can towards your knees. You're aiming for a relatively straight diagonal line from knees to bust/shoulders. Hold for 5-10 seconds and then lower and repeat. You'll notice that this exercise also works your butt muscles.

The last exercise is a clamshell or sideways frog. Lay on your side with your knees bent to 90 degrees in front of you and your feet roughly in line with your torso. Bend your bottom arm up to support your head. To do the exercise, you want to lift your top knee upwards by rotating outward at the hip and keeping your feet together. Lift/open as far as you can, hold for a few seconds, then lower back to the starting position. Repeat 10-20 times per side, again gradually working up with the number of repetitions as you get stronger.

Most OBs will also have handouts with home exercises you can do, so reach out to your doctor for additional resources.

Low-Impact Exercises and Weight Training Modifications

Until your pelvic floor gets stronger, you want to avoid doing things that place it under increased pressure. If you haven't noticed already, activities like jumping and running often make prolapse more uncomfortable.

As you begin to become more active, it is important to stick with primarily low-impact activities like walking, biking, and swimming (after being cleared by your OB). If you enjoy exercise videos or classes, make sure to step instead of jump or otherwise modify the moves to minimize bouncing—and if the class is in person, ask the instructor for suggestions.

Strength training can also cause issues for prolapse. This is because lifting something heavy increases the pressure inside your abdomen, which in turn increases the pressure on your pelvic floor from above.

In addition to avoiding maximal/very heavy weights, the best strategy is to find exercises that work the muscles you want to work but are performed sitting or lying down.

Lifting Workarounds

Lying down is great for, say, doing a chest press. But what about when you need to lift your two-year-old out of their crib? The reality is that although you can minimize the amount of lifting you do, unless you are under post-surgery restrictions from a c-section, you will end up doing some lifting. The key is to lift as little as you reasonably can and to lift in ways that will best protect your body.

- Have your toddler crawl into your lap and then stand up instead of leaning over to pick him up.
- Avoid carrying heavy objects (including tiny humans) up and down the stairs. There isn't much work-around for up, but coming down, you can give a younger child a "butt scoot ride."
- Collect laundry from each bedroom separately instead of piling them all together.
- Pack the grocery bags less full and let someone else make that warehouse club run.
- Carry anything relatively heavy as close to the body as possible, and use good body mechanics by squatting up and down instead of leaning over whenever possible.

Hair Loss

"*Everybody said my hair would fall out after my daughter was born. The first couple of months, nothing. I thought maybe I'd escaped the curse, but alas, it was not to be. One day, I was washing my hair, and it started coming out almost by the fistful. I didn't want to clog up the drain in the tub, so I pulled it off my hands, stuck it to the shower wall, and kinda forgot about it. My husband got home from working out and went into the bathroom to shower. I was nursing our baby when my phone chirped. He'd turned the smear of hair into art—the face of a bearded man on the tile wall, to be specific! I just about died laughing, but I haven't forgotten to clean up my shedding even once—and I've had two more kids since then.*"

—**Dana, 41, mama of three**

So, what is hair, really?

Basically, hair is a long string of dead cells that are filled with a hard protein called keratin. Glamorous, right? But hair cells don't start out as dead. They're alive when they form in the hair follicle under the skin on your head. But when they get pushed upwards and out of the skin, they get squished and lose their blood supply. As this happens, they fill up with a protein called keratin that makes them hard and strong. The dead and dying cells keep getting pushed towards the surface by the still-healthy cells forming underneath. And thus, hair grows.

Every hair on your body has its own growth cycle. The first phase is called anagen. This is where your hair is actively growing as described above. This phase lasts anywhere from 3 to 7 years for the hairs on your head. In someone with normal, healthy hair, around 90% of the individual hairs are in anagen at any given time.

After anagen comes catagen—a transitional phase during which hair growth slows and the body prepares to shed the hair. At this point, the hair stays in place but detaches from the bottom of the follicle. This transition takes about ten days.

After catagen comes telogen—a resting phase where the body pauses the whole process. The hair is sitting in the follicle, but it isn't growing. It doesn't usually fall out, though, provided you're in good health. Telogen usually lasts about three months.

The last phase is the exogen phase—where the individual strand of hair falls out, and a new one starts to form in the follicle. This shedding phase lasts several months. Most healthy people lose 50 to 100 strands of hair daily, which is a lot if you think about what's in your hairbrush.

After the hair falls out, the whole process repeats itself. On average, hair grows at about six inches per year. This varies a bit from person to person, with race being one of the bigger contributors. Women of Asian descent tend to have faster hair growth, and women of African heritage tend to have slower hair growth. This has to do with hair type and follicle angle—the way the strand of hair comes out of your head. There's some support that hair may grow faster in the summer months, but this isn't a big enough change for us to notice.

Pregnancy and Hair

One of the positive changes to your body during pregnancy is your hair. Increased estrogen and testosterone levels during pregnancy cause hair to stay in the growth phase longer—which means that the number of hairs in the growth phase increases, and the number of hairs falling out decreases.[1] Often, your hair becomes shinier, too! The downside? That increase in hair growth isn't limited to the hair on your head. The interesting thing about hair is that we want more of it on our heads and less of it everywhere else. So, while the extra hair growth on your head is great, the extra hair growth everywhere else may send you scrambling for a razor. [3]

Why do we lose our hair after having a baby?

Increased hair growth in pregnancy is caused by high hormone levels; when your hormone levels return to normal after delivery, so does your hair. In other words, all those hairs that were supposed to have stopped growing and moved into catagen and telogen while you were pregnant are now doing just that. If you include the hairs that are reaching this point naturally, it all adds up to a lot of hair now in the loss phase.

But this change doesn't happen immediately. It takes time for your hormone levels to drop. And you'll remember that catagen and telogen take time, too. This is why it's usually several months after delivery before your hair starts falling out. And this is also why it seems like the hair loss process continues for longer than it should, especially with the fluctuating hormone levels associated with breastfeeding and when you start having regular periods again.

What else can contribute to hair loss?

According to the American Academy of Dermatology, postpartum hair loss should peak around four months and return to normal by one year[4]. This is the "normal" cycle for hair loss related to changing hormone levels and the physical stress of delivery. If you're still losing excessive amounts of hair after that point, it's time to consider whether something else could be causing your hair loss.

For many women, there are multiple issues that can contribute to overall hair loss. These issues include physical and emotional stress, poor diet, hair treatments (dyes, perms, and chemical relaxers), hairstyles (ponytails, tight braids, use of hot styling tools), medications, and certain medical conditions like thyroid problems.[4]

How does stress affect hair loss?

Physical and emotional stress is one of the most common contributors to post-baby hair loss. Giving birth is stressful. Having a newborn is even more stressful. Even with a good support network, your sleep is suddenly fragmented, and your daily routine has been turned upside down. Telogen effluvium is the name given to this stress-induced hair loss.

When you are under stress, your body increases certain stress hormones. These hormones cause your hair follicles to enter or stay in the resting phase, instead of staying in the growth phase. The net effect is a prolonged resting phase and less hair growth. Within a few months, these hairs then enter the shedding phase and fall out when brushing or washing your hair. [1]

According to the American Pregnancy Association, the official incidence of postpartum telogen effluvium is around 40-50%. This means that your likelihood of stress-induced increased hair loss during the first six months post-delivery is about the same odds as getting heads on a coin toss. [3]

What other health problems can cause hair loss?

There are a few different medical conditions that can cause hair loss. The most common of these is thyroid problems. The thyroid is a small organ in your neck that helps to regulate metabolism through the production of thyroid hormones. Both too much and too little thyroid hormone can cause hair loss. Because changes in the level of thyroid function can happen after delivery, it's essential to be checked out by your doctor if you have severe or prolonged hair loss. Symptoms of thyroid problems to look for would include constipation, racing heartbeats, swelling in the neck, and heat/cold intolerance (see Chapter 14 for more details on thyroid problems.) Medications to normalize thyroid hormone levels will also cause hair loss to improve or resolve entirely over several months.

One type of anemia, in which you have low blood counts due to low iron levels, is also related to hair loss. Treatment, usually in the form of iron supplements, will help. But even if you were told your blood counts were low after delivery, don't rush out and start taking iron on your own! Using iron supplements has to be monitored, as taking too much can cause iron to build up in your body. Many nutrients are dumped out in the urine if you take too much. Iron is not one of them and too much iron can build up in the body, and have consequences. So, if you were told you were anemic or think you might be, please make an appointment with your doctor for blood work. If your levels are low, you'll receive instructions on what to do next.[5, 6]

Many autoimmune conditions are also associated with hair loss. These conditions also typically cause joint pain, swelling, and/or skin rashes. Although you can develop an autoimmune disease during or after pregnancy, it's much more common to have received these diagnoses at another time in your life. So, if you have one of these conditions, be aware that the changes happening to your body after giving birth can cause your disease to flare up, and follow up with your care team. If you don't have one of these conditions and you have new joint pain, swelling, and/or skin rashes, please see your primary care doctor or a rheumatologist for further testing.

Could my itchy head be causing hair loss?

Certain skin conditions can also cause hair loss. These range from chronic medical problems like psoriasis to acute skin infections like ringworm. If you notice a rash on your scalp, or if your head starts to itch and you're getting a "bald spot" instead of just overall thinning of your hair, then a skin condition could be causing your hair loss. Most skin conditions require treatment by a licensed professional, so you should schedule an appointment with your primary care doctor or a dermatologist to be evaluated for one of these causes of hair loss.

Does what I eat affect hair growth?

Absolutely! The cells that are responsible for hair growth, just like those on the skin's surface and the lining of your intestines, are dividing almost constantly. Any time the body goes through continuous growth, you need certain vitamins and minerals to support that growth. Your body also needs enough protein and fatty acids to support hair growth.

Very low-calorie diets—like we see for weight loss—can cause hair loss for multiple reasons. Not only do they often contain too little of the things your body needs for hair to grow, the big drop in calories causes stress on the body. For most of human existence, a large drop in calories meant famine, which equaled major stress on the body just to survive. When under stress, the body will send all of its resources to the things that matter most for survival—and that is not your hair.

What should I eat to help my hair?

First, eat enough. We all want to lose the baby weight as soon as possible. We all want our old bodies back, a common but perhaps unrealistic goal for some of us. Not eating enough calories is surprisingly common, and as noted above, it will impact hair growth. Adequate protein intake is also necessary, but in this country, even if you are vegan, average protein intake typically far exceeds the RDA (recommended daily allowance) minimum. Did you know that a serving (0.5-1 cup) of many fruits and vegetables contains at least a gram of protein? True. A cup of blueberries has 2g, actually. And two cups of raw kale has 4g! So, if you have a bowl of oatmeal, a cup of berries, and a couple of tablespoons of nuts or seeds, you can easily consume 10-12g of protein—or more—without touching a sausage patty.

Second, make sure you are getting enough healthy fats. Including healthy fat in your diet is important for more than just breastfeeding. There are some suggestions that omega 3 fatty acids—whether as DHA/EPA (docosahexaenoic acid/ eicosapentaenoic acid) from fish and algae or as ALA (alpha lipoic acid) from flax, chia, and walnuts—are beneficial for both hair growth and hair health in general. Although the data comes from supplement use, the recommendation is to take the supplement with a fat-containing meal. So why not just eat the food and get the benefits of all the other nutrients, too?

Biotin is the most well-known vitamin associated with treating hair loss. It can stimulate keratin production, but it also plays a role in the follicle growth rate. Animal sources of biotin are usually touted by nutrition professionals and include egg yolks and meat, especially organ meats. Vegetable sources, however, can also provide high levels of vitamins and include legumes (beans), nuts and seeds, sweet potatoes, nutritional yeast, bananas, avocados, and broccoli.

Zinc is another vitamin that is associated with hair loss. It helps give strength to the hair follicle and plays a role in DNA formation, making it valuable for growing cells. Its role in DNA formation is why it's essential for healing wounds. Zinc deficiency has also shown some association with early graying, and correction can sometimes lead to restoration of hair color. Foods high in zinc include meat and seafood, especially oysters, dairy, and eggs. Vegetarian sources include beans and whole grains, though there is disagreement about how much of the zinc can be absorbed from non-meat sources. In the U.S,. breakfast cereals are also usually fortified with zinc, making them a significant source of the vitamin.

Selenium is the last nutrient that has been linked to hair loss. Selenium is a trace mineral, meaning that our body requires and stores only minimal amounts, but it's essential to bodily functions. The catch is that both too little and too much selenium have been implicated, although the high levels required to produce hair loss are unlikely to be achieved without significant effort on your part. Due to high selenium levels in the soil and fortification of many cereals, selenium deficiency is relatively rare. Common dietary sources of selenium include meats, seafood, eggs, brazil nuts, whole wheat bread, beans/lentils, and rice. [2]

What about supplements for hair growth?

There are dozens of supplements available claiming to prevent or reverse hair loss. Current medical research suggests that they are mostly ineffective and may even be harmful by causing too-high levels of one or more nutrients. For example, very high levels of selenium can cause massive hair loss, similar to what you see in chemotherapy. Excess iron intake can cause liver and other organ problems. Excess zinc intake can cause deficiencies of other minerals like copper and magnesium. Supplements containing only B vitamins can lead to imbalances if the ratios between the individual vitamins are not similar to those required by the body. For those reasons, I do not generally recommend supplements unless your doctor has tested your blood levels and found them to be low.

What about hair care?

The things we do to our hair in the name of beauty are not always best when it comes to the health of our hair. Coloring, perming, and relaxing treatments all put stress on the hair. Heated styling tools and hair dryers damage the individual strands of hair. Sometimes, a particular shampoo can cause issues. Tight hairstyles like braids and ponytails with tight elastics can sometimes lead to hair loss. As most of us tend to do less with our hair when we're juggling caring for a newborn, this is usually not the sole cause of hair loss. It can, however, contribute to hair loss and is worth considering when determining what you can do to support and care for your hair.

When should I seek medical care?

The typical pattern for postpartum hair loss is that it starts 2-4 months after delivery, lasts for 3-6 months, and then gets better gradually. If you have hair loss that persists past that point or is severe, seeing your doctor is recommended. Likewise, if you have symptoms of an underlying medical condition, as I described earlier, you should see a doctor. If you have scalp problems like itching, rashes, or patchy hair loss, these also suggest a separate underlying cause for your hair loss and should be checked out.

Otherwise, try to breathe deep, be patient, and give your hair a little extra TLC. Your hair will not fall out in handfuls forever. As time passes, this issue will become just a memory, and someday, you'll look back and laugh about the whole situation.

Toolkit

Chia Pudding

There's nothing better than starting your day with a fast and easy—and delicious—breakfast! Enter chia pudding. Packed with healthy omega 3 fats, antioxidants, and fiber, chia seeds are a nutritional powerhouse that can keep you full all morning.

I like to make my chia pudding the night before and let it sit in the fridge overnight to thicken, but you can make it the same day. If you do the latter, be aware that you will either need to let it sit and chill for an hour or two to thicken, or blend it up in the blender to make chia mousse. The mousse form is also great if the tapioca-like texture of regular chia pudding is a turn-off for you.

- Combine 2 tbsp chia seeds with ½ cup milk of your choice. We love oat milk but any kind of milk will work. Add a hint of sweetness with 1 tsp maple syrup or honey. I also like to add ½ tsp of a high-quality vanilla extract (not the imitation stuff).
- Stir the ingredients well in a bowl and let them sit for about ten minutes to start to thicken. Then, give them one more good stir to make sure you don't end up with crunchy clumps in your pudding. Finally, transfer the mixture into a container (I like to use the smaller glass canning jars) and put it in the fridge overnight. When you get up in the morning, the pudding will have thickened. Give it one last stir, add extra milk if it's thicker than you'd like, and enjoy!

- Chia pudding is good plain, but it's even better with a few toppings. Adding things like fresh or frozen berries, chopped nuts, or even a couple of teaspoons of cocoa powder can really amp up the flavor. I'll admit that I've even made chocolate chia mousse for my kids and called it "dessert" without complaints!

And one of the best things about chia pudding is that it keeps in the refrigerator for four or five days, so you can double or triple the recipe easily and only prep once or twice a week!

Caring for Your Fragile Hair

Unless you are routinely doing numerous things that are hard on your hair, I don't suggest a major change in hairstyle—unless of course you've found that your old hairstyle isn't very compatible with your new mom life. This is a distressing but transient stage in our lives, so it's usually easier to do what we can to minimize the damage without making major changes. A baby is enough change.

- If you routinely wash your hair every day, try decreasing it to every other or every third day.
- Let your hair air dry instead of using a blow dryer, if possible.
- If you use a hair dryer, flat iron, or curling iron, invest in a heat protectant product to put on your hair before heating it—this helps to protect the strand of hair itself.

My biggest struggle was to avoid automatically putting my hair in a ponytail or messy bun every day. I was so tired, and it was the easiest way to make my hair presentable. Even with a fabric scrunchie instead of a thin elastic, the pressure on the hair follicle from pulling your hair back can accelerate hair release. The same is true for braids and other tightly bound styles.

Best ways to clear a slow shower drain/best hair catchers:

The thing about hair loss is that the hair inevitably ends up in places you'd rather it didn't—namely, down the drain, on your bathroom floor, and wound up in your vacuum. So, here are a few tips to help you deal with the inevitable fallout.

Get a hair catcher for your shower drain. If you have a tub/shower combo, they make raised soft plastic ones with tiny suction cups on the bottom. These look like tiny, wide-brimmed hats. The hat part has small holes to let the water pass down, not the hair. If you have a shower stall with a flat drain, OXO makes a stainless steel disc with holes and rubber edges that will sit over the drain.

If you already have a slow tub (or sink) drain, I find that the best—albeit most gross—way to solve the problem is to get one of those long plastic sticks with the little tines on either side and push it down there in a few different spots and pull the hair out. Wear gloves and have a few paper towels to collect the hair you pull out for disposal in the trash. There's an "ew" factor for sure, but it's usually quick and efficient and a lot less expensive than commercial drain cleaners.

With that said, if your drain is still slow, you should use a commercial drain cleaning product and follow the directions precisely. Make sure to run the vent fan and open a window because most of these have a strong bleach odor.

Ways to manage hair on your floors:

Nothing makes a mess of the roller on your vacuum like long hair. Most of the time when you have carpet in your home, you can't see that your hair has fallen on it. So, I recommend periodically looking at the roller on your vacuum to see if it needs to be cleaned—you'll find it works much better!

If there is a lot of hair in there and your vacuum roller is not easy to remove (or doing so doesn't help you), I recommend an inexpensive tool to help—a seam/stitch ripper for sewing. These usually cost a couple of dollars, and you can usually get one at Walmart or Target in the laundry or sewing/crafting sections. Be careful; the tip is very sharp! Insert it under a tight band of hair and then push. It will easily cut through the hair so you can pull it out.

For hard surface floors, investing in a dust mop with a reusable cover is a fast and easy way to lift up the hair, and any dust bunnies, without having to bend over or take out heavy cleaning tools.

Body Shape Changes

"Nobody has ever compared me to a pixie. I'm tall; I've got big bones. Even before babies, I wore a size 9 shoe. Cute shoes, too. Designer shoe clearance racks were my jam. Towards the end of my pregnancy, they started to pinch my toes, but I chalked it up to the marshmallow man toes I had from the late summer super pregnant swelling. After my son was born, I was home on maternity leave, so I often went barefoot. The swelling went away, but it got replaced with this awful pain on the bottom of my feet—like little men with hot pokers stabbing me. I finally gave up and went to the doctor. He told me I had to wear good, supportive shoes all the time. I was less than excited until I realized he'd just given me permission to go shoe shopping."

—Tracy, 33, mom of one

Why does my body change so much during pregnancy?

The short answer is because you're growing a tiny human inside it, of course! The reality is that a lot needs to happen for your body to take on the extra job of supporting a baby inside it. You need to make space for this little one to live. You need to get enough nutrients to the baby through your blood. And once you've grown a baby to the point where they can survive without being attached to you, this little person has to exit your body. No easy feat these days, with birth weights and gestational diabetes rates climbing higher and higher.

The overall driver of most changes is something called ligamentous laxity. Ligaments are thick and relatively inflexible bands of connective tissue that hold our bones together and in proper alignment. When you sprain your ankle, you stretch and tear part of the ligament that holds two of your ankle bones together. Think of them like a well-worn pair of jeans. They move easily within their allowed range, but if you try to push them further, they rip. During pregnancy, your ovaries make a hormone called relaxin. This hormone causes your ligaments to become looser. As the baby grows and takes up more space in your pelvis, the looser ligaments allow the pelvis and hip bones to spread out to give your baby the space it needs.

Unfortunately, the body can't pick and choose locations to loosen up ligaments. Relaxin circulates through the blood. So, while the ligaments of the pelvis loosen to accommodate your growing baby, the ligaments in your arms, legs, and back loosen up, too. This is part of why pregnant women are at higher risk for falls and injuries—the joints aren't as stable as they were.

Why do I have so much trouble with my feet since giving birth?

One of the most common effects of pregnancy is perceived foot growth. Your feet don't actually grow, but they seem to. Shoe size—and shoe width—often go up because the ligaments holding the bones of your feet together loosen up. This causes the bones to spread farther apart, and the arch in your feet may fall. Many women will go up about a half size in their shoes during pregnancy. Compound that laxity with increased time going barefoot around the house before and after delivery, and it sets women up to develop a painful foot condition called plantar fasciitis, which is tendonitis of the bottom of the foot. In addition to pain with standing and walking, plantar fasciitis also causes pain in the bottom of the foot when you first stand up after sitting or lying down for long periods of time.

The number one thing to do for plantar fasciitis is to stop going barefoot. Your feet need support. If you have a pair of lace-up tennis shoes in your closet, put them on in the morning and take them off at night. Start to ice and stretch the bottom of your feet. One of the easiest ways to do this is by using a frozen water bottle. Simply sit on the sofa and roll the arch of your foot back and forth over the frozen water bottle (please wear a sock!). Do this for at least 10-15 minutes, at least twice a day.

Over the counter medications like ibuprofen and naproxen are helpful for the pain because they decrease inflammation. An anti-inflammatory diet (low in sugar and free of processed and high-fat foods) can also be helpful, as can anti-inflammatory herbs and spices like cinnamon, turmeric, and ginger. But for safety reasons, if you are considering anti-inflammatory supplements or homeopathy, you should check with your provider for guidance.

What other body shape changes could I see?

Your rib cage will expand during late pregnancy as your baby pushes everything else up out of your pelvis. Women with smaller rib cages notice this the most, although the change is usually painless. Many women will go up a band size on their bra. If you look at nursing bras, you will notice that they often have more than two or three sets of hooks. Immediately after delivery, your rib cage is still spread out from pregnancy. With time, however, the rib cage usually compresses back to its pre-baby size.

The other significant change women notice is in the lower back and hips. In order for our bodies to carry and deliver a baby, the bones of our lower back and pelvis need to spread out and the ligaments relax. For some women, this increased mobility isn't a problem. For others, it can lead to significant back and hip pain.

"I'd never had back pain in my life until after my second pregnancy. Whether it was the way my son was positioned, or hidden effects from my delivery, I don't know. But the pain kept me from sleeping and riding in the car. When it didn't go away, my OB sent me to physical therapy, which helped some. Then I saw one of his partners who was an osteopathic doctor and worked with my back to get me the rest of the way to normal."

—Maureen, 31, mama of two

Traditionally, allopathic medicine has shunned osteopathic and chiropractic manipulation. Over the last five years, this has begun to change as research studies have been published suggesting benefits for a variety of pain conditions. Postpartum back problems are typically multifactorial, involving lingering laxity, weak core muscles, and malalignment from delivery. For that reason, a treatment approach involving multiple different interventions is most useful. Physical therapy and yoga can strengthen core and surrounding muscles and help relearn proper posture. Ultrasound stimulation, TENS unit, and massage can help with spasms and muscle tension. And manipulation can help with malalignment.

Are these pregnancy-related changes permanent?

The answer is sometimes. If you have gone up a half or whole size in your shoes, it's probably permanent. If your feet are now very flat, that's often permanent, too. On the upside, it's a nice excuse to buy cute but comfy new shoes for your new mom life. Conditions like plantar fasciitis are treatable and often go away, but may come back months or years down the road.

Increased rib cage size usually decreases within a few months of delivery to return to normal. Occasionally, very petite women will have a permanent change. When I had my first son, my band size went from a 32 to a 34. It has never gone back down. Personally, I'm okay with that because it makes bra shopping at major retailers much easier.

The changes in your hips, pelvis, and lower back are much more variable. Not everyone gets them to a noticeable degree, and they aren't necessarily permanent. In fact, the vast majority of them typically do resolve within two weeks of delivery. The pelvic spread at the pubic ligament (which holds the two sides of the front of the pelvis together) usually mostly resolves. Still, if there is damage to any of the ligaments holding the back and pelvis together, which is rare, you can have pain lasting 6-12 months or more.

When to seek professional help?

For most women, these changes can be irritating but not necessarily life-altering. If you have significant pain in your feet, back, or hips, please see a healthcare provider and get evaluated. If you have shooting pain down your legs or arms or numbness and tingling, these aren't normal and need to be examined. The same goes for joints that crack, clunk, or don't work the way they need to work. If it impacts your ability to sleep or live your daily life, it's a concern. Having a baby does change your body. It does not mean that you should have constant pain or problems.

There are treatments available for plantar fasciitis, ranging from medications to injections to custom inserts. Back and hip issues can often be managed through stretching and strengthening exercises and other care, as noted above. Medications can be used as well. Over the first few weeks after delivery, your body will gradually feel more familiar to you. If something doesn't settle right, there are medical professionals who can help you feel like yourself again.

Toolkit

How to Shop for Good Shoes

One key to finding the right shoes is to know your foot or walking type. The easiest way to do this is by walking barefoot with wet feet across concrete or somewhere you can see your footprints. When doing this, you look at the middle part of the foot where the arch is. Specifically, you are looking at how wide the print is at the arch. A very narrow print up the outside of the foot means you have a high arch. A wide print with almost no unprinted area means you have flat feet. Somewhere in between means you have a normal footprint, which is considered "neutral" at most shoe stores.

If you have high arches, shoes with extra cushioning and adequate arch support are key. Sometimes, a low heel is more comfortable than a flat heel. Over the counter inserts made for high arches are also a good option.

If you have flat feet, shoes that support the inside of your foot and keep you from rolling inward (called pronating) are especially important. If you are able to go to a shoe store with a salesperson, ask for a shoe with "pronation control." Over the counter inserts specially made for flat feet/pronation can also sometimes be helpful.

Superfeet is a brand that sells specialty inserts for different activities and foot types. Their website has an excellent tool that walks you through which style (each style has its own color, making it easy to remember) will most likely be right for you.

How to Measure Yourself for a Bra

According to lingerie stores, most women aren't wearing the right size bra. We usually have too big of a band size and too small of a cup size. Pregnancy and nursing make bra selection challenging at best. Although it is tempting to live in nursing tanks for months, having a good, supportive bra is essential for having your clothes fit right—and for feeling good about yourself and how you look.

So, you can go to your favorite lingerie store to get measured, but a lot of women would rather measure themselves in the privacy of their own homes and then order online. Step one is to get a soft plastic tape measure or even a piece of string. Wear a thinner, unpadded bra that isn't a compressive sports bra. Measure around your rib cage right under your breasts. Add 4 to the number if it's even and 5 if it's odd. This gives you your band size. For example, if you get 31.25 inches, your band size is 31+5 or 36. Then, measure around the fullest part of your breasts. Look at the difference between the two numbers. One inch = A, two inches = B, three inches = C, etc.

Fun things to note—in terms of the actual volume of your breasts, a 38B is the same as a 36C or a 40A. It's all about how the volume is distributed, aka whether your breasts are narrow-based and stick out more, or broad-based and stick out less. So, if you find that your mathematical size doesn't fit, try going up or down using this pattern.

To Nurse or Not to Nurse—That is the Question

"I knew from the beginning that I didn't want to breastfeed. Not that I didn't want my baby to have all the nutritional benefits, but I knew I couldn't handle not being able to tell if he was getting enough to eat and wondering if he was crying because he was hungry or for some other reason. My husband and I had been together since high school, and when the pediatrician at the hospital started pushing me, he told her that his wife's mental health mattered more for our son than what kind of milk we fed him. I love him and how he stood up for me in that moment. And nobody has questioned me since."

—Beth, 26, mama of one

"It never occurred to me that I wouldn't breastfeed. I'd wanted kids for what felt like my whole life and always dreamed of being a mother. And growing up in rural Eastern Europe, everybody breastfed. When I came to the U.S. on scholarship, I was surprised to see that things weren't the same here. But when my daughter was born, that didn't affect my choice to nurse."

—Natalia, 25, mama of one

How does the body make milk?

Along with pigs, cows, and many other animals, humans are classified as "mammals"—a group of beings that feed their young by producing their own milk in mammary glands. In cows, these are the teats that are milked by a farmer. In humans, these are your breasts.

When you are pregnant, your estrogen and progesterone levels go up. This causes the milk ducts in your breasts to grow, which in turn causes your breasts to become fuller. Often, your nipples will also get darker in color, and your areola (the dark-colored area around the nipple bud) will also get bigger. Later in your pregnancy, you will start making colostrum, the special kind of breast milk that your baby eats the first few days of life.

The labor process stimulates the production of a hormone called oxytocin, which helps milk flow in early breastfeeding. The rapid drop in estrogen and progesterone levels and initiation of nursing trigger increased levels of a hormone called prolactin, which tells your body to increase milk production. The more time your baby spends nursing and the more milk is removed from your breasts, the more milk your body makes. Eventually, this cycle takes over and becomes more independent from prolactin. At this time, hormone levels usually decrease—without affecting your milk production.[1]

Why does breastfeeding hurt so much? Does it ever get any better?

For most women, early breastfeeding hurts. The nipples are a very sensitive area of the body, and now your baby is smashing them and yanking on them every couple of hours. Sometimes, pain can be a sign of a problem. If your baby isn't latching on properly (usually, this is not getting enough nipple into the baby's mouth), breastfeeding can be very painful. But sometimes, even a "good" latch can cause pain. My oldest son had a very strong suck. I remember sitting in the rocking chair nursing him at 2am with tears rolling down my face from pain and exhaustion. Typically, the nipple sensitivity starts to improve after the first week or two. With my first baby, it took around three weeks, but with my second it was much faster. By four to six weeks of nursing, most women have no pain at all.

What can I do to help with the pain?

First and most importantly, get expert help from a lactation specialist to ensure that all of the mechanics of breastfeeding are happening properly.

Then, load up on lanolin (an ointment safe for baby to ingest—remember they're going to be sucking on this skin), cotton bras, and warm washcloths. Your breast milk also has powerful healing properties. Hand expressing a few drops of extra milk and then rubbing it over the entire nipple area can help heal and prevent skin infections.

If the pain does not improve, or if you develop pain after breastfeeding without pain for a period of time, please get expert help. This can be a sign of a blocked duct, milk duct inflammation or infection, or a skin infection. If your skin is firm, red, and warm, or if you have a fever, this is more likely to be the case. See the next chapter for help troubleshooting common breastfeeding issues. If your infant starts eating poorly and cries more frequently, your baby could have thrush and have given you an associated yeast infection on your nipple. Both should be treated as soon as possible.

For many women, once they get past the initial period of sensitivity and the early logistical challenges, breastfeeding can be a wonderful way to nourish and bond with your baby.

If it hurts so much in the beginning, why do women choose to breastfeed?

There are a lot of benefits of breastfeeding, both for you and your baby. First, there is the power of colostrum, the milk produced by your breasts for the first few days of life. Colostrum is a special kind of milk that contains high levels of protein, nutrients, and antioxidants to help your baby thrive in the first few days of life. It also contains high levels of immune globulins (antibodies) to help protect your baby against infection and help your baby develop healthy gut flora.

Second, according to the CDC, breastfed babies have lower risks of asthma, type 1 diabetes, obesity, and sudden infant death syndrome (SIDS). They also get fewer stomach bugs and ear infections.

Third, breastfeeding decreases your risks for breast and ovarian cancer later in life, as well as lower rates of diabetes and high blood pressure. Not to mention that the added energy required to produce breast milk often translates into easier postpartum weight loss.

Fourth, it helps you bond with your baby. The skin-to-skin contact and nursing relationship helps your baby feel safe, secure, and loved. Although mamas and babies can gain cuddle time and bonding outside of breastfeeding, nursing is an automatic "pause and be close" button to help strengthen the relationship between us.

What if I don't want to breastfeed my baby?

That's okay. As a medical professional, I encourage all women to strongly consider attempting to nurse—at least for the first few months. The reason for this is that a lot of medical research indicates that babies who consume breast milk (as opposed to formula) have lower rates of allergic and asthmatic conditions, decreased odds of developing diabetes, and lower childhood obesity rates.

What I don't encourage is judging or shaming a woman who chooses not to breastfeed. It breaks my heart to see this happen, and I cannot tell you the number of times I've spoken up on social media to defend a fellow mama from abusive posts about her choice not to nurse.

We all have our own road. If you struggle with anxiety and fears about your baby getting enough to eat can be all-consuming. Some women can pump to manage these worries, others cannot. If you are a single parent of multiple children, the sheer time difference it takes to nurse versus bottle feed can be challenging. If you work two jobs trying to make ends meet, you may not be able to pump enough during the workday. Despite laws otherwise, I will tell you that even working in healthcare, the pressure to "pump as quickly as possible and get back to work" can be overwhelming. With my second son, I was traveling around between nursing homes. The irregular schedule meant I had a power converter to run my pump off my car and a cooler to put the milk into. There is nothing like pumping in your car in Minnesota in the middle of winter. Brrrr… Unsurprisingly, my milk production suffered.

My point is that we all have our own roads, and some women have the reserves and social support to move mountains to be able to nurse. Others do not. Instead of resorting to social media backlash, we should be offering love and support regardless of how a fellow mama has chosen to raise her child.

How do you "dry up" milk production after delivery if you choose not to nurse?

If you have chosen not to breastfeed, your milk will still come in a few days after delivery. It usually will not be as impressive as someone who's been breastfeeding a newborn every two hours, but it will happen. First, wear a comfortable, supportive bra. Your breasts will be swollen, heavy, and sore. There's no point in being extra uncomfortable to look nice or save a few dollars on a throwaway stretchy bra. Do not wear a tight sports bra or otherwise bind your breasts; this increases the risk of developing mastitis.

Make sure you have some soft, non-rigid ice packs—or label a small bag of frozen peas or corn. Apply them to your breasts for 5-15 minutes at a time every few hours. Make sure to have a cloth between the actual ice pack and your skin to prevent freezing your skin!

Try chilled or frozen cabbage leaves! It sounds weird, but research suggests that there is some benefit for both breast pain and swelling with the application of cabbage leaves—and they're the perfect size and shape. Take a few large leaves off a head of cabbage and either refrigerate or freeze them until they are very cold. Then, tuck them into your bra around your breasts and leave them there. Replace as needed. Easy!

Avoid hot showers or warm compresses. This feels counterintuitive. Shouldn't your sore, swollen breasts feel better with these treatments? Absolutely. But there's a big catch: these things increase milk production and can stimulate milk letdown and release, which is counterproductive to your goal of drying up your milk supply.

Although there is a lot of chatter on the internet and in mom's groups about herbal treatments, there is no clear support in the research that these things are helpful. That said, drinking a cup or two of peppermint tea daily is unlikely to be harmful. Ditto for putting a little fresh sage in your chicken bake. However, based on the available information, I would avoid oils and high-dose capsules. You can take over-the-counter analgesics like Tylenol or Motrin as needed for breast pain. They will not entirely relieve the pain but make it more bearable until your milk production drops.

Hand expression of a small amount of milk to relieve breast pain, is also okay within reason. The idea is to decrease your pain to tolerable levels without telling your body to produce a lot more milk by stimulating your nipples and removing a large amount of milk from the breast (which your body will then try to replace because it thinks your baby just ate and will be coming back for more).[2]

Toolkit

If you are on the fence about breastfeeding, here are a few questions to help you consider the best path for you and your family. If you are still undecided, know that you can always start—and then decide to stop. Although possible, it's much more difficult to change your mind the other way.

1. Are you considering exclusively breastfeeding or exclusively bottle feeding, or would you be open to doing some of both?
   - Pros to a hybrid approach include flexibility and decreased feeding stressors from work schedule and/or life events
   - Cons include potential for infant taste preferences impacting intake and possible impacts on milk supply

2. Do you work outside the home? If so, do you want to breastfeed while working?
   - Legally, employers are required to give women access to break time and a place to pump. However, the logistics of what is available to you at your workplace may influence your decision.
   - Do you have access to a breast pump and supplies?
   - Do you feel strongly enough about breastfeeding to navigate any feelings of guilt or pushback from coworkers about pumping?

3. Do you have a strong family history of conditions that can be helped by breastfeeding (for you or baby)?

4. Are you willing and able to be the primary food supplier for your baby?
    - Do you have any medical conditions yourself or take any medications or supplements that could be unsafe for your baby?
    - Do you have the emotional bandwidth to be the around-the-clock food source—or are you willing to pump or supplement with formula?
    - Does your partner feel strongly about being involved in feeding your baby? If so, are you willing/able to pump to give them that ability?
5. Are there strong family/cultural predispositions that you will have to navigate if you make a certain choice?
    - This is not to say that you should not have free choice, but acknowledging that certain paths may be easier based on your own upbringing and that dealing with family members who disagree with your choice can be stressful.

Breastfeeding Woes

"I wish someone had told me beforehand how hard breastfeeding was the first month! I spent so much time and energy beating myself up about it—how I was a lousy mom and a lousy woman. Then, out of the blue one day, my older sister says how much she admires that I didn't complain about it and how she was miserable for six straight weeks when she was trying to breastfeed my nephew before he suddenly got the hang of it. I looked at her like huh, you mean it's normal for my nipples to burn and my boobs to ache and for it to take me like six tries to get my baby to latch properly? She just laughed, and I felt this huge sense of relief wash over me. I wasn't a failure after all. I was just a normal mom with a normal baby."

—**Hailey, 33, mama of two**

How am I supposed to hold my baby while breastfeeding?

There's this assumption that, as women, we intuitively know how to breastfeed a baby. And the baby will magically know how to nurse—just like a baby cow. The reality is that when you're just starting out, breastfeeding is hard! There's a whole new language to learn and a learning curve for both you and your baby. So, if you have no clue what to do and everything feels awkward, know that you are not alone.

There are about a dozen (maybe more) potential breastfeeding positions. Some of these are much more common—and more comfortable—than others. The cradle hold is what most of us associate with breastfeeding, but it can be tough if you need a hand free to help your baby to latch on. So, someone came up with the cross-cradle, where you tuck your baby in one arm which leaves the other hand free to manipulate your breast and help your baby to latch.

The other common positions are laid-back (when you're laying on your back semi-reclined and your baby is on top of you), side-lying (laying on your side with your baby lying on the bed and eating from the lower breast), and the football hold (your baby is tucked under your arm at your side, like a running back carrying a football). A friend and I had a good laugh about the last one, because, really, what woman would've named that position? If you are searching for more information about possible nursing positions, the La Leche League is an excellent resource for all things breastfeeding-related.

Experts recommend that you use more than one different breastfeeding position. One reason to do this is that when your baby nurses, the entire breast doesn't drain the same. Usually, the area of the breast across from where the baby's chin is located will be drained of milk more effectively than other areas. If you notice that you are getting a firm area on your breast, one way to manage this (in addition to compresses and massage) is to change positions on the next feeding so that this area will get drained better.

What do I do if my baby seems to be having trouble breastfeeding?

If you have any concerns about how your baby is nursing, talk to a doctor right away about getting a visit with a lactation consultant. Often, this can be arranged by your OB or your baby's pediatrician, and it is typically covered by insurance.

There are a lot of reasons why a baby can struggle to nurse. Some of these are related to physical issues on the baby's side. Lip tie and tongue tie are the most common. In both situations, there is an abnormal tissue connection in the mouth. In tongue tie, the thin attachment you see on the underside of the tongue is either too thick or extends too far forward and affects the baby's ability to stimulate the nipple and suck. A lip tie generally refers to the upper lip, but a lower lip tie can happen, too. In this case, the attachment holding the lip to the upper portion of the gums (called the frenulum) is too thick or too tight, and it prevents full movement of the lips, causing problems with latching on and sucking.

Sometimes, there are physical issues on your side as well. Some women have variations in how their nipples look—either flat or inverted. These types of nipples can make it more difficult for your baby to latch on and start to feed. If you have one of these nipple types, please be assured that most babies are still able to breastfeed in either situation. The key to breastfeeding success with different nipple types is having a lactation consultant see you at the time of delivery or shortly thereafter, certainly before you and your baby are discharged from the hospital. These experts can help you and your baby learn to breastfeed successfully most of the time.

Anatomy aside, the biggest reason babies don't nurse well (or that breastfeeding is very painful) is an improper latch. This refers to how the baby's mouth is positioned on the breast. It's important for your baby to get enough of your nipple into the mouth and to have the lips and tongue positioned properly. Failure to do so can result in ineffective feeding for the baby and a lot of pain for you. This is another situation where a lactation consultant can be valuable in teaching you how to help your baby eat properly.

There are other, less common reasons your baby may struggle to breastfeed. If you've worked with lactation without success, then it's very important to follow up with your pediatrician for further assistance.

How do I know if I have mastitis or just a blocked milk duct?

Mastitis, by definition, is simply inflammation of the breast—that's what an "-itis" is. We often use it to mean a breast infection, but reality is more complicated than that. Think of a line—a continuum or spectrum. At one end, you have a firm, sore area of your breast due to overproduction of breast milk or the beginnings of a blocked milk duct. At the other end, you have a full-blown bacterial infection with a fever of 102 degrees, flu-like symptoms, and a red, hot, swollen area of your breast so tender that you can hardly stand the pain.

The best way to help yourself as a breastfeeding mama is to take good care of your breasts. During the early days, when sleep is a premium, it's tempting to forgo self-care in favor of an extra ten minutes of rest. But if you can make a little bit of extra effort, your body will thank you. Start by using a safe topical nipple balm to prevent cracking. Make sure your baby has a good deep latch and isn't chomping on your nipples. Use multiple different breastfeeding positions to ensure you drain the whole breast regularly. Avoid wearing tight bras or tops that compress the breasts. And when you are ready to discontinue breastfeeding, do so gradually.

Another key to prevention is to know your breasts well and to monitor for these slightly sore and firm areas. Or the larger and more firm areas, a little tender, and perhaps slightly red. This is where you can do good self-care and decrease your chances of progressing to the point where antibiotics are necessary.

When you find one of these areas, your goal is to get the milk flowing through and out of it as soon as possible. There are several steps you can take to help your body. First, apply a warm (not hot) compress to the area for 5-10 minutes before nursing your baby. This will help open up the ducts and soften the breast. Make sure your baby eats from the problem breast first. Adjust your breastfeeding position so that this area is across from your baby's chin (remember, that's the spot that gets drained the best). After your baby eats, if you still have significant firmness, try pumping—or get in a warm shower, massage the area, and hand express milk.

Much of the time, these simple steps will help rapidly resolve the problem area. Within a day or two, you can go about your normal life. Sometimes, the area will worsen. It will become bigger and more tender, and the skin overlying it will turn red. If these things happen, or if you start to feel ill or run any low-grade fever, then it's time to call your doctor so they can determine whether you need antibiotics. Although, you want to avoid unnecessary antibiotics; mastitis can get worse in a hurry, so you should pay attention to your body with the same care you use to watch over your baby.

When you have mastitis requiring antibiotics, you usually can (and should) continue to breastfeed. This is because the bacteria causing the infection usually come from your baby's mouth and aren't likely to make your baby ill. If you end up needing an antibiotic that isn't safe for nursing, usually due to medication allergies, you should pump and dump to avoid a drop in milk production.

What's the best strategy for pumping?

The best pumping plan depends on your goal. Are you pumping due to the inability to nurse your baby while at work, or are you pumping as a replacement for breastfeeding directly due to personal choice or other issues (yours or your baby's)? How much of an extra stash do you want to have in the freezer?

If you are pumping because you want to give your baby breast milk exclusively (or almost exclusively) and you are unable to nurse for technical reasons (anatomy or your baby is still hospitalized), then you want to pump just like if you were breastfeeding. From birth, every couple of hours, around the clock. And you want to pump enough milk per session for an entire feeding, if possible. If you want to try to build up an extra supply of milk in the freezer, you will need to start pumping more milk than the amount you need to give your baby per feeding or pumping in between feedings to save.

If you are not pumping due to an inability to breastfeed directly, then the big question is whether or not you are trying to build up an extra supply of breast milk in the freezer. If you are not, then you will simply be pumping at the feedings that you cannot directly nurse your baby (whether you are at work or otherwise physically away from your baby). If you do want an extra stash, you will want to do extra pumping sessions while nursing your baby.

Whether you want a freezer stocked with breast milk or not, most women are successful when they start pumping within 2-4 weeks of birth. Earlier is usually better, but many factors go into that decision, and discussing it with your doctor and your pediatrician is the best option. If you are trying to build up an extra supply of frozen breast milk, you will do one or more extra pumping sessions daily. Many women can successfully pump immediately after their infant is done eating. Other mamas, like myself, have babies who happily gulp down their entire milk supply. In this situation, pumping about an hour after nursing is another option. This strategy works best when you have more than two hours between feedings, as your breasts need time to fill up again after pumping. Either way, you're unlikely to get an entire extra bottle of milk every time you pump—unless you have a stellar milk supply. In this situation, milk from multiple pumping sessions can be combined to make a whole "serving" to freeze.

Why doesn't the breast pump remove as much milk as my baby does?

This is a common complaint among women returning to work and pumping for multiple feedings in a row. There are a number of reasons this can be the case.

First, sometimes the "standard" size flange (the funnel-looking piece that goes on your breast) isn't the right size for your body. Second, sometimes the pump doesn't produce as much sucking force as your baby—at least not in settings you can tolerate. This was my problem with my firstborn. Although I had a baby with a powerful suck, my tolerance for pumping was much lower. I fought this constant battle of turning the pump strength up and down based on how sore I was versus how far I was from reaching the number of ounces I needed.

Both those things aside, the most common issue related to getting enough milk when pumping is failing to get a true "let down." The letdown reflex is that moment when your nipples suddenly get firm, swollen, and tingly, and then milk starts coming out on its own. Many women have experienced this when they hear a baby crying and then look down and see milk stains on their shirt, but it happens when you're breastfeeding, too. If your baby is an eager eater, they may choke on the sudden rapid flow of milk. Breast pumps have a special setting to try and mimic a baby's first sucks to trigger that milk letdown. Usually, the pump runs for 1-2 minutes at a faster rate, then cycles down to a slower rate. The machine assumes you've had letdown by then, but news flash—sometimes you haven't! If you haven't felt or seen that sudden rapid increase in milk return when you hear the machine slow down, that's your cue to punch the buttons to re-run the fast cycle until you do. Discovering this was a game-changer for me.

I also discovered that when I was feeling stressed out or rushed, it was much harder to get that letdown to happen. I literally had to coach myself to sit, close my eyes, and breathe deeply. Breastfeeding is part of the whole feed or breed nervous system, and it gets suppressed when you're stuck in fight or flight mode—regardless of why you're there. One coworker told me she would shoot videos of her baby on her phone to watch while she was nursing. She felt like it helped her pump more milk. She was right. Think briefly about what resonates with you—what ideas can you try?

What foods affect breast milk production?

Although a lot of attention is given to things that promote milk production, there are several things that decrease milk production that should be discussed first. Because caffeine is a diuretic (meaning it makes you urinate more often), anything that has caffeine in it can decrease milk supply by dehydrating you a little bit. That means coffee, many teas, and sodas all have the potential to impact how much milk you make. In fact, soda can be a double whammy because carbonation can also impact milk production. The key here is to look at quantity—a single cup of coffee vs three cans of Mountain Dew—and your response. Some people are more sensitive than others. If you're struggling with supply and you consume caffeine, try cutting it down or out entirely for a few weeks and see what happens.

Foods that can decrease breast milk are relatively few because the quantity required to have an impact usually exceeds what most normal people consume. That said, mint or peppermint is one to be aware of, particularly if you are a gum chewer. Many women also consumed peppermint teas when pregnant because they were caffeine-free and helped with digestive upsets. In this case, substituting another caffeine-free herbal tea is strongly recommended, especially in the early stages of breastfeeding while you are still trying to establish your milk supply. The other herb to remember is sage, but unless it's Thanksgiving or you have a thing for breakfast sausage, you probably aren't consuming enough to have a significant impact.

Water is the number one thing you can consume to help your milk supply. Lots and lots of water. Preferably at least 70-100 ounces a day, depending on your body weight (higher weight = more water), activity level (more active = more water), and if you consume any caffeine (yes = more water). As noted in our discussion on skin, a majority of people are chronically mildly dehydrated, so the general rule of thumb is that you probably need more than you are currently drinking.

One way to get more water is to start the day with a big glass of water (12-16oz). As soon as you get up and walk into the bathroom, fill a big glass of water and drink it as you get dressed and make your bed. Not only will you be filling up your body's tank to start the day, but you'll find it makes you more alert.

Water aside, there are several foods that also help with milk production. Whole grains have been shown to be beneficial, with oatmeal being the star grain. Oats contain multiple compounds—everything from iron to saponins to healthy plant estrogens—that are associated with greater milk production. Other whole grains like barley, quinoa, rice, and cornmeal also give benefits.

Nuts and seeds also have a positive impact on milk supply, with almonds generally considered the most beneficial in this group. They contain multiple minerals as well as healthy proteins and have been shown in research to have a positive impact on milk production.

When it comes to meat, chicken and turkey are the most beneficial due to their protein content and high levels of an amino acid called tryptophan. Considered a "calming" substance, tryptophan is one of the building blocks in the production of prolactin, which is the hormone that controls milk production.

What about all those breastfeeding cookies and teas? Do they work?

Over the last ten to fifteen years, there has been an explosion of products marketed towards nursing women. Everything from disposable nursing pads to books, fancy drapes, and yes, breastfeeding cookies can now be purchased. As to whether any of it is worth your money, the answer is that it all depends.

Most of these cookies, biscuits, and other food items usually contain one or more of the beneficial foods noted above. Some taste pretty good; others have a decided aftertaste or gritty texture. Some of them aren't too bad for you, and others contain large amounts of sugars and chemicals. They are moderately expensive, but if finding time to bake your own only adds to the overwhelm, the cost may be worth it.

When it comes to lactation teas, most of them are made up of multiple herbs with variable evidence to support the benefits of breastfeeding. Fenugreek, fennel seeds, and anise are some common ingredients. For those of you who aren't familiar with Middle-Eastern cooking, fenugreek tastes like sweet celery. Fennel and anise both have a distinct black licorice flavor. If these are not flavors you find appealing, you may want to stick with other beverages.

The take-home message? Most of these products contain substances that are thought to possibly be helpful for breastfeeding. Regarding medical research, there is some data to support the benefit from fenugreek. Otherwise, there isn't a lot of data out there. That said, there is good reason to believe that the foods I've named may have some degree of benefit. If you are struggling with milk supply and you don't have the desire to put together your own foods to try, I would advise sticking with products that don't have added sugars or manufactured ingredients you cannot recognize or pronounce. Test a product for a couple of weeks at a time and take notes on your milk production to have an unbiased answer regarding whether something works for you.

What if my breasts make too much milk?

Although oversupply is less common than undersupply, some women do struggle with having a larger milk supply than they want or need. Much of the time, early oversupply evens out by six weeks as your body starts to naturally regulate your milk production with your baby's eating habits. However, some women will continue to make more milk than needed.

Symptoms of oversupply include firm, swollen breasts and feeling like your breasts refill before your baby is due to eat again. Your baby may have trouble latching on initially because your breasts are so full or may gag due to larger amounts of milk being released under higher pressure. Sometimes, your baby gets diarrhea due to drinking mostly the thinner early milk as opposed to the higher-fat milk released later in a nursing session.

Managing and correcting oversupply is a delicate balance and talking to a lactation consultant about your individual situation is a good idea. If you want to begin trying to decrease your milk supply on your own, there are a few things you can do.

First, stop pumping excess milk. Many women want a freezer stash. Most don't want their milk to take over their food storage space. An empty breast is what triggers your body to make milk. If your breast is still mostly full after a feeding, it will only signal your body to make a small amount of milk.

Second, feed your baby by alternating breasts. Start with the right side and let your baby eat from that side until satisfied. This will allow your baby to get the good, fat-rich milk that is at the "bottom" of the breast. If your baby is still hungry, switch breasts. Otherwise, hand express or pump off from the left breast only what you need for comfort. Then at the next feeding, the baby starts from the left side and eats until satisfied and you hand express or pump from the right breast. Usually, feeding in this manner for a few days will start to have a significant impact on your milk production. When this happens, your baby will start wanting to eat from both breasts during feeding. This leads to developing a natural balance between milk production and your baby's individual nutritional needs.

A third option exists as well. If you have a local hospital or other organization that accepts pumped milk, you can choose to donate your excess breast milk. In this scenario, you feed your baby from alternating breasts and pump fully from the "unused" breast, donating the pumped milk.

> *"Several years ago, my nephew was in the NICU and got donor milk. When my daughter came along, and I had more breast milk than I knew what to do with, my sister suggested that I give it to the hospital. It was a bit of a process initially, but it made me feel so good to be able to give back to the place where they had taken care of him."*
>
> —**Sandy, 25, mama of one**

What if I can't breastfeed?

Deep breath. It's okay. Some women have medical conditions requiring medications that are not safe for breastfeeding. Others have social situations that do not allow for it. Sometimes, there is a "technical" issue, like your baby being in the neonatal intensive care unit or having a tongue tie or birth defect affecting their ability to nurse. Or maybe you have an uncommon nipple structure that makes it hard for a baby to latch on and nurse.

There are a lot of women who try to breastfeed only to discover that they can't. Several of my friends went through this, nursing around the clock and thinking they just had fussy babies who didn't want to sleep. Then those first pediatrician visits showed problems gaining weight. Eventually, this led to the discovery that their breasts didn't make enough breast milk. These women were doing everything right, and it didn't matter.

In some ways, this is a harder situation than when you are choosing not to breastfeed because it's your own body preventing you from nursing. One woman told me, "I feel like a failure as a woman because I can't nurse my own child. It's like I'm broken; I'm not a 'proper' woman because my body doesn't provide the nourishment my baby needs."

I know it's easier said than done, but please try not to beat yourself up. We all have our own unique health quirks—that doesn't make some of us better than others. Give yourself a hug. Confide in your significant other or a trusted friend. You are beautiful, and there is nothing wrong with your body. You can still love your baby and raise a healthy baby without breastfeeding. Millions of women do it every day.

Toolkit

Comparison of Pump Brands

If you are going to breastfeed, you will usually want to have a breast pump—a device you can use to remove milk from your breasts when you are unable to feed your baby directly. If you do not plan to pump except occasionally, a good manual pump will often suffice at a fraction of the cost. But if you will be pumping on a regular basis, you'll likely want an electric pump of some kind. If you have health insurance coverage for a pump and want to use it, you may have a shorter list of options to choose from.

Here are a few of the most commonly available pumps:

1. Medela—one of the oldest and most reputable pump companies is Medela, and they have several options that many women love. Their hospital-grade pump (the Symphony), which I had access to when pumping at work, was remarkably efficient without being more uncomfortable. If you are pumping exclusively, some women will opt to rent a hospital-grade model. They also have a "regular" pump that is well-rated and a newer hands-free model (the Freestyle), which is becoming more popular.

2. Spectra—one of the top choices in most online surveys and my favorite (non-hospital grade) pump was the Spectra. The biggest perks are the digital adjustable settings, ability to recharge the battery (S1) and get a car

adaptor, and overall comfort and ease of use. The large handle design also makes it easy to move from place to place.

3. Elvie—the original Elvie is still the top-rated wearable pump in most surveys. It's quiet, discrete, and uses reusable storage containers instead of plastic milk bags. The biggest downside is the cost, which is fairly steep, and the fact that you do have to be upright and a little careful about positioning to ensure you keep a good seal. Willow is one of the other big names in wearable hands-free pumps.

4. Motif—this little pump packs a lot of suction in a small and lightweight pump, making it easy to move around the house, particularly if you get the battery-powered option.

5. Momcozy—if you're looking to try a wearable pump but want to avoid the cost of an Elvie or a Willow, consider giving Momcozy's wearable pump a try. It's a little more cumbersome and a little louder, but a lot easier on the pocketbook, particularly if you only need to use it some of the time.

6. Haakaa—unlike the brands above, Haakaa is best known for their manual pumps. Specifically, they are known for their silicone manual pump. A single piece of food-grade silicone, you simply squeeze the collection bulb and place it on your breast. Many women use it to collect a few ounces of extra milk while nursing on the opposite side. It's inexpensive and easy to clean as well.

Compresses and Other Things

There are a lot of products out there that can make your journey a little smoother. There are far more gadgets and gizmos than any woman needs, but some of them are more likely to be helpful than others. Here are a few of my favorites:

Booby Tubes: these are hot/cold packs that come in a spiral shape. Use them cold for engorgement or comfort when weaning. Use them warm right before nursing to relieve mastitis or help with milk supply.

Nipple Ointment: choose one with baby-safe lanolin and apply a pea-sized amount to your nipples after feeding for the first month or two to help soothe sore nipples and prevent cracking and mastitis. The jars look small, but a little goes a long way!

Microwave Sterilizer Bag: if you pump more than once at work or a big round plastic sterilizer takes up too much space in your kitchen, this is a great solution. Basically, this is a large ziptop bag made of silicone or special plastics (I prefer the silicone) that you put your supplies in after washing and microwave for a set period of time to kill all the germs.

Nursing Tanks: find one you love that fits you well and stock up. These are basically camisoles with shelf bras and strap clips, and they are great for keeping you comfortable and covered when feeding. Working in the hospital, I would put one under my scrub top, and then when it came time to pump, I would take off my germ-covered scrub top without feeling too exposed (or freezing cold).

Lactation Bites

A lot of commercial lactation products are marketed as cookies and frequently contain as much sugar as a regular cookie. This recipe is more similar to an energy bite that you might consume before or after exercise. Why an energy bite? By cutting out the baking time, they're infinitely faster to prepare. They're lower in sugar to keep your mood and blood sugar stable. And most importantly, because they're delicious!

Ingredients

- 1 c rolled oats (not quick cook or instant oats)
- ½ c flaxseed meal (available in most grocery stores)
- 2/3 c almond butter ("natural" kinds you have to stir are thinner and mix better)
- 4-5 tbsp pure maple syrup
- ½ tsp vanilla
- ¼ c mini chocolate chips
- ¼ c chopped craisins

Mix the oats and flax in a big bowl. Mix the wet ingredients (almond butter, syrup, vanilla) in a smaller bowl until well blended. Then, add the wet mixture to the dry mixture and stir well. When they are well combined, add in the mini chips and craisins. At this point, it is easier to put a little oil on your hands and mix by hand, and it is more fun. Once things are all mixed up, chill the mixture briefly to make it easier to handle. Then, roll it into little (1-1.5in) balls. The balls can be kept in the refrigerator for up to a week or in the freezer for up to three months.

Coping With the Exhaustion

"I fell asleep on a plate of spaghetti, just like they show in cartoons. Well, maybe not quite that messy. But still. It was pretty ugly. My son had been struggling with colic for weeks, and my preschooler had croup, and I can't even tell you how long I'd gone without a decent rest. My husband was talking to our daughter, and the next thing I remember, my face felt weirdly wet. My daughter thought it was hysterical and wanted to eat the sauce off my face. Me? I was just grateful I had my hair in a messy bun on my head."

—Olivia, 34, mama of two

What happens when you go to sleep?

The sleep cycle is regulated by your body's innate 24-hour circadian rhythm and by specialized neurons (nerve cells) in your brain. Your body has natural rhythms for everything from sleeping to eating to activity. These are automatic and regulated by bright light exposure. In addition to those natural rhythms, we have nerve cells in our brain that help to regulate how alert versus how drowsy we are. These neurons run from your brainstem, which controls breathing and most things we don't think about, and your cerebral cortex, which controls most of our thoughts.

The neurons are regulated by chemical messengers called neurotransmitters and by hormones like melatonin. When you sleep, your brain responds to messages to turn off the parts of your brain that keep you awake. At first, this seemed backward to me. How could I feel so tired if my brain's default status was awake? But the key is understanding that the chemicals responsible for turning off the brain build up gradually during the day, increasing as daylight fades to darkness.

Once you fall asleep, most people enter NREM (non-rapid eye movement) sleep. This type of sleep has four different phases, with each phase representing progressively deeper sleep. About three-quarters of your night is spent in some level of NREM sleep. The rest of the night is spent in REM (rapid eye movement) sleep. This is the type of sleep where most of your dreams happen.

After you fall asleep, you progress through the four stages of NREM sleep and then transition into REM sleep. After an episode of REM sleep, the entire cycle repeats. The first cycle is the shortest and usually lasts about 70 minutes, which is why taking a one-hour nap often makes you feel more tired instead of less. If you're a mama who's already gone back to work and is struggling with that morning alarm clock, try setting it ten or twenty minutes earlier to catch your body earlier in the sleep cycle. It sounds counterintuitive, but you may find it's a lot easier to get out of bed that way.[1]

Sleep physiology is one of the reasons that caring for a newborn feels harder than the absolute number of hours you sleep. Getting up to feed your baby every two hours means you never fall into that rhythm of repeating sleep cycles. It also means that you're often awakened in one of the stages of deeper sleep when you feel more lethargic, trying to shift your brain into wakefulness.

> *"One of the best ideas my husband came up with to help me after I returned to work was for us to alternate nights getting up with our son. One night, I would get up for both feedings. The next night, it was his turn. It was a complete lifesaver to get that full night of rest every other night."*
>
> —Nicole, 36, mama of one

Sleep?! I can't sleep. What if something happens to my baby?

Having a newborn baby can feel scary, especially if it's your first baby. Because I wasn't blessed with babies who slept well, I was typically exhausted enough to sleep regardless. However, several of my friends and a few of my patients struggled with just this issue. With your baby cozy in his tiny bed in your room, you may find that instead of blissful sleep, you lay awake listening to his breathing. Every little noise, every little pause, may send you running to his side to make sure he's okay.

Although it's not frequently discussed, the American Academy of Pediatrics recommends having your baby sleep in your room for the first six months of life. Not in your bed, of course, but in their own crib, bassinet, or co-sleeper. And the well-known recommendations for sleeping on their back without any bedding are also still true. Many parents struggle with the idea of having their newborn in their bedroom for this long, but the research supports that 90% of SIDS cases occur before six months and that having the infant sleep in the same room as the parents reduces the rate of SIDS.[2]

The best strategy to decrease worry and increase sleep is to try to calm your mind. Focus on visualizing your baby waking up happy and well-rested. Manage your own mind by using deep breathing exercises, meditation apps, or even taking a hot shower or bath before bed. If you're otherwise healthy, supplements like magnesium and low-dose melatonin can also be helpful. Just stay away from Tylenol PM and other sleep medications containing Benadryl or similar medications if you're breastfeeding, since these can decrease milk production.

I'm so exhausted that I'm nodding off while feeding my baby in the middle of the night. I'm so scared I'm going to drop him—how do I keep myself awake?

This is a common problem during the first few months when the nighttime feedings are frequent, and you're so sleep-deprived that your body's protective signals are battling your conscious will to stay awake. Please don't give in to the temptation to get comfy and close your eyes for a few minutes as your baby eats. Accidental entrapment in sofa cushions, between a mattress and the wall, or against a parent is one of the top causes of infant death.

So, how do you stay awake? You've got to help your conscious brain override the sleep signals. The best ways to do this involve engaging either your mind, your body, or both. Things like moving your body, eating, breathing in certain ways, watching funny shows, and listening to upbeat music can all help you to remain awake and alert while feeding your baby in the middle of the night—or anytime, really.

> *"Oh my gosh, I'm going to pull my hair out. It's 10am and my baby just fell asleep, and all I wanted was to crawl back into bed and sleep for a few minutes. But no, MY brain starts running in circles at a million miles a minute. It's like somebody infused it with Red Bull. And the more I toss and turn, the worse it gets until I finally give up and get out of bed again. I just want to be able to take a nap!"*
>
> —**Nadine, 27, mama of three**

Why can't I fall asleep when I lay down to take a nap?

The first question to ask yourself is how much caffeine you've consumed and when. Nadine hadn't actually had a Red Bull, but her brain felt like it. Some lucky people are rapid metabolizers of caffeine. You know the type—they can have coffee or an energy drink in the evening and lay down and fall asleep. Others are like me, slow metabolizers. If I have a cup of coffee after 11am, I can forget about going to bed early. Most people are somewhere in between on this spectrum. Think about life back before pregnancy (seems like a lifetime, huh) and try to identify where you fall on this spectrum.

Although those two cups of coffee you had at 7am are partly to blame, caffeine is only part of the story. Chronic sleep deprivation turns up the sympathetic nervous system—the one responsible for the fight or flight reaction you learned about in high school biology class. The chemicals produced by this reaction generate adrenaline-like responses. Imagine a large crash waking you up in the middle of the night. Even if you verify there's no burglar in your house—it was just the shower curtain rod falling down—how easy is it to fall back asleep? Exactly.

There are simple tools you can use to turn down the adrenaline response and fall asleep more easily. These tools range from a warm shower/bath to breathing exercises and include certain yoga poses, tai chi, and movement practices. Special kinds of music can also be helpful.

The final thing that can help you (and your baby) to nap better is to get yourselves into a predictable daily routine. Sleep comes easier for everyone when your body is accustomed to sleeping and waking at certain times. This is why you wake up at 6am on a Saturday, even without setting an alarm clock. Most of the time, your baby's sleep-wake cycle dictates your available nap times. Keep track of feeding/eating/sleeping times for a few days and see if you notice a pattern, then try to stay on a more predictable schedule. This doesn't mean you need to feed your baby at exactly 10:00 am, no matter what. It does mean that at 9:45, you should start paying attention to see if your baby is getting hungry. And if you don't see any hunger cues by 10:15ish, you should consider offering food and seeing how your baby responds. Some babies always seem hungry, others don't seem to care, but regardless of their outward behavior, all babies need to eat regularly, especially for the first six months of life before solid foods are introduced.

Once your lives are in a more predictable routine, you can decide when you want your own rest times to be. You'll find after a week or two of consistent rest times, your body will calm down as rest approaches and you'll wake up easier at the end of the nap.

Can't I just take a sleeping pill?

The use of sleeping medications when you have an infant is complicated. These medications make you drowsy, so it's harder to wake up if your baby starts crying. You may also be lethargic when you awaken, which can impair your ability to care for your baby once awake. If another adult is present, taking medication to help with sleep—prescription or over the counter—is a reasonable option.

Breastfeeding further complicates your ability to use sleeping medications. Most prescription medications have unknown safety profiles for breastfeeding. Over the counter medications like Tylenol PM are safe but can affect your milk supply. Occasional use is often tolerated, but regular use is not recommended for this reason.

The only time I can get anything done is while my baby is sleeping. How can I find time to take a nap?

This was my default refrain for far too long, especially with my second baby, and women with three or more children say it just gets stronger. As women, we tend to put ourselves last. Self-care gets pushed aside when there is something to be done for the kids, the house, your spouse, your job, and your friends. And you can keep going on fumes for months or even years. But sooner or later, you'll run out of gas in your own tank and find yourself depressed, discouraged, defeated, and unable to care for anyone.

Even knowing better, I was guilty of this for a long time. I'd push off things I loved, needed, and even basic self-care, until I started to feel thin and frayed around the edges. There isn't an easy fix, but I'll tell you what motivated me to change. I noticed that when I was feeling thin and frayed, I couldn't be the mama I wanted to be. I was short-tempered, less affectionate, and less attentive to my family. Some days, I just didn't even care. All I wanted was for them all to go away and leave me alone. Anybody relate? And that doesn't mean that you don't love your little ones. It just means that you need to fill your own tank first. Like the safety warning on an airplane, you need to put on your own oxygen mask before assisting others with theirs.

If I'm taking the time for sleep and other self-care, how do I keep up with everything that needs to be done?

Well, sometimes you've just got to redefine "needs to be done." There is this societal perception that we, as women, should be able to care for our kids, hold down a full-time job, have a gorgeous house, throw Pinterest-perfect parties, and be thin and fit and beautiful at all times. Does anybody else look through social media and feel the overwhelming pressure to do more, be more? I saw this struggle in my female patients long before I became a mama and lived it myself. And let me tell you, the stress of trying to live up to society's idea of a "perfect" woman is exhausting—and impossible.

And it's also unfulfilling. If you're an introvert, you have no desire to have a dozen people over for a dinner party. If you're not into exercise, going to the gym feels like torture. Why put ourselves through all that? Becoming a mama is the perfect reason to take a step back and consider what you really value, and what you'd be happy to let go of. Authenticity is an amazing gift you can give your little one.

The second way to keep up is to enlist the help of your family and friends. The old adage "it takes a village to raise a child" has never been more true. Except that the framework of modern society no longer supports that ideal. Households in most cultures are not multi-generational. Here in the U.S., most women are expected to return to work just 6-8 weeks after giving birth. And those 6-8 weeks off may not be paid. Many women live far from extended family, and even close friends may be a 30-60 minute drive away. We are too caught up in our own overscheduled, technology-dependent lives to be outside long enough to connect with our neighbors.

Creating your own village can be sanity-saving. For most women, this starts with having an honest conversation with your significant other. Not in an accusatory "you don't help around the house enough" kind of way, but in an "I'm drowning and can you help me figure out a solution" kind of way.

Who makes up your village is as unique as your fingerprints. Think about the people in your life, their talents, and how they make you feel. If your mother-in-law makes you nuts, ask her to do things like make you a casserole, pick up your drive-up order, or take the baby for a walk so that you can shower in peace. Your kid brother may be terrified of babies but willing to mow the lawn so that your spouse can help you indoors. Generally, people genuinely LIKE to help others. It makes us feel good.

Am I ever going to stop feeling like a zombie?

Although it seems like the severe sleep deprivation phase will last forever, it doesn't. Somewhere around 3-6 months, most babies will be able to sleep through the night. Even before that time, as your newborn gains weight, you will be able to space out feedings so that you're no longer getting up every two hours all night long. Although sleeping through the night is ideal, most women notice that getting down to just one overnight feeding made a big difference in how they felt the next day.

Toolkit

Five tips for those moments when you're nodding off and you need to stay awake:

1. Put on a favorite, upbeat song
2. Eat or drink something
3. Anything cold (air in your face, ice pack, ice cubes or cold shower if you're feeling really brave)
4. Phone a friend or family member (talk to someone, anyone)
5. Try an essential oil or scented candle—sweet orange, peppermint/spearmint, and rosemary are especially good for energy and focus

Five tips for those moments when you want to sleep and can't:

1. Have a cup of herbal tea
2. Keep your screens off
3. Listen to binaural beats or meditation music
4. Close your eyes and think about all the things you're grateful for
5. Try box breathing. This breathing pattern has proven benefits for stress, anxiety, and sleep. The idea is that you breathe in a way that your breath forms a box. Breathe in for three seconds (count one-two-three; you don't have to actually time it). Then hold your breath for three seconds.

Then exhale for three seconds. Then hold your breath (your empty lungs) for three seconds. Then repeat. The first few breaths, you may only be able to do 2-3 seconds per phase, but as your mind and body slow down, you should be able to lengthen that to 4-6 seconds per phase.

Five tips for organizing life and keeping your commitments reasonable:

1. If you don't already, do one load of mixed laundry every 2-4 days instead of waiting until you have three or four loads that need to be sorted. Today's detergents are good enough that most things can be washed together on cold and then dried on low unless the label says otherwise. And one load of laundry to hang and fold is so much more manageable than three.

2. When you cook dinner, make enough to have the same meal again (or at least the main items) in a few days. Although we all think about this for chili and stew, you can do it for most meals that you will prepare. Yes, this requires you to meal plan. The benefit is that when dinner time rolls around, and you're too exhausted to think about what to eat, you don't have to.

3. Get used to saying, "let me check and get back to you tomorrow," when asked to do anything. The physical and mental separation gives you time to evaluate whether you want to do the item and whether you have the bandwidth to do it.

4. Revisit what you (and your partner's) priorities are for this new season of life. Recognize that for the next six months or more, your reserve is not going to be high and that for the next several years, life is going to be very different from the way it was before. Decide what you want your priorities to be for this season, and keep them in mind when deciding how to spend your time.

5. Make a list of family and friends who can help with daycare and errands, and note when they are usually available. When you get overwhelmed or when you find yourself getting stressed about an obligation or unexpected problem, reach out to your list for help.

Beyond Exhaustion

"Initially, I thought this was just the way it was supposed to be. Everybody says you're supposed to be tired, and I was. I was so exhausted that all I wanted to do was curl up under a warm blanket ALL the time. One day, I was rubbing lotion into my neck and felt a couple of lumps. Like, my heart stopped. I looked in the mirror. Actually looked, you know? Not just looked without seeing, but actually looked at my neck. It was HUGE! Like a weird mutant turkey neck. I called my doctor and she got me in for blood work and an ultrasound. After a few days of medication, I started to feel so much more normal. And my neck did gradually go back to looking like my neck again, too."

—Carrie, 38, mama of one

Could something other than lack of sleep be making me feel so exhausted? I know I'm supposed to be tired, but this is just ridiculous…

Several medical conditions can develop after giving birth that can affect your body's ability to function normally. One is anemia. If you had increased bleeding when your baby was born, or if your body's iron and vitamin stores are low because you couldn't tolerate prenatal vitamins when you were pregnant, you can develop low blood counts (also called low hemoglobin or anemia). Generally, this makes you feel more fatigued all the time. You also may find that you can't tolerate exercise or activity as much as you used to, and people may say that you look pale.

You can also develop postpartum thyroid and heart conditions that can lead to severe fatigue and other symptoms. Because these conditions can be life-threatening, it is very important to see your doctor if you have (what feels like) unusually severe fatigue or any of the other issues discussed below.

How is my thyroid supposed to work?

Normally, the brain sends a chemical messenger to the thyroid gland called TSH (thyroid-stimulating hormone). This tells the thyroid gland to make more thyroid hormone—called T4. The more TSH the brain sends, the more T4 the thyroid makes. Pretty simple right? Except that T4 is a pretty weak version of thyroid hormone, so when it gets released into the blood, some of it will get converted into a stronger thyroid hormone—called T3. This mostly happens in the liver but also in the muscles, gut, and some organs. There are special sensors in the brain to detect how much thyroid hormone is in the blood so the body knows how much to tell the thyroid gland to make.

The active thyroid hormones (T4 and T3) are carried throughout the body in the blood and control your body's metabolism. That means they can affect your weight, body temperature, growth, and energy, as well as things like digestion and heart rate.

When your body doesn't have enough thyroid hormone, you can get low energy, dry skin/hair/nails, constipation, cold intolerance, heavy periods, and weight gain. When your body has too much thyroid hormone, you can get anxiety, racing heartbeat, sweating, diarrhea, heat intolerance, hair loss, tremors, irregular periods, and weight loss.

As you can see from these lists, the symptoms of thyroid problems are common and not very specific, which is probably why the American Thyroid Association estimates that a whopping 60% of Americans with thyroid problems are unaware they have the condition. Postpartum thyroiditis—the most common thyroid problem after pregnancy—represents about 5% of all thyroid conditions and often also leads to swelling and discomfort in the front and sides of the neck where the thyroid is located, in addition to some of the other symptoms.

Why would having a baby affect my thyroid?

During pregnancy, your thyroid activity usually increases because your body is metabolically working harder. It's growing a baby, after all. This means that the thyroid gland itself is working much harder than it has been to produce higher levels of thyroid hormones to help your body support the growth of your baby. Usually, things rapidly return to normal after your baby is born. Except that sometimes they don't.

There are several reasons that your thyroid can malfunction after delivery, the most common of which is postpartum thyroiditis, affecting about 3% of women in the first year after delivery. This means that your thyroid gland becomes inflamed (-itis means inflammation in medicine). As noted above, the inflammation can give you swelling and tenderness at the front of the neck, where your thyroid is located. With the inflammation, your overall thyroid hormone levels can be high, low, or normal. We don't fully know for certain why this can happen.

You can also develop autoimmune thyroid disease. Although more than half of women with postpartum thyroiditis have at least one type of thyroid antibody on blood tests, many do not. And although some women with autoimmune thyroid disease get thyroid inflammation, others do not. In autoimmune thyroid disease, the body forms antibodies that interact with the thyroid gland. These antibodies can either suppress your thyroid gland or stimulate it, depending on the type. Some women probably had the antibodies at low levels prior to pregnancy without knowing it, and others developed them after delivery.

The third reason you can have thyroid problems after having a baby is that the part of the brain that regulates thyroid hormone production can become damaged during delivery, so your brain isn't telling your body to make enough thyroid hormone anymore. This is very uncommon (about 0.005% of women), and unlike the first two examples, which can give you high or low thyroid levels, this one only gives you low levels. It also usually causes other symptoms like lack of breast milk, lack of periods, low blood pressure, and loss of pubic hair.

How long do postpartum thyroid conditions last?

For postpartum thyroiditis, the good news is that in more than 80% of cases, it resolves within one year. Some women's symptoms and lab findings are mild enough that they don't even require treatment, just frequent lab monitoring. Other women will need treatment, which usually involves medication taken by mouth daily to either help with the effects of too much thyroid hormone or to replace low levels by supplementing with prescription thyroid hormone.

For women who have type 1 diabetes, a history of thyroid antibodies, or a family history of thyroid problems, postpartum thyroid conditions can sometimes become permanent. If this happens, long-term use of medications and lab monitoring will be required.

What do you mean by postpartum heart conditions?

Even if you are otherwise young and healthy, you could develop a rare medical problem called postpartum cardiomyopathy. This affects somewhere between 0.03% and 0.1% of women. In this condition, your heart starts having trouble pumping the way it should. When the heart doesn't pump properly, it can affect the amount of blood that gets to different parts of your body. This can cause you to retain water. This usually happens gradually over a period of days to weeks. It makes you feel very fatigued and often causes problems with ankle swelling and shortness of breath, especially when lying down or with physical activity.

Postpartum cardiomyopathy can lead to acute heart failure, which can make you sick enough to need hospitalization or even threaten your life. Because of the serious nature of this condition, it's important to see a doctor promptly if you have symptoms like these.

Although postpartum heart problems are very rare, there are certain things that increase your risk, such as age over 35, being of African descent, having twins, having at least three previous pregnancies, high blood pressure, living below the poverty line, and a history of drug use. Even knowing these risk factors, the precise cause of a woman's postpartum cardiomyopathy is usually unknown. Unlike most forms of cardiomyopathy, which are related to heart disease, heart attacks, or certain medical conditions, there is no clear identifiable cause for most cases of postpartum cardiomyopathy.[1, 2]

What if I develop postpartum cardiomyopathy? Will it ever go away?

The honest but frustrating answer is maybe. About half of women with postpartum cardiomyopathy will have improvement in their heart function with treatment—often within three to six months. Treatment usually consists of taking medications to help the heart muscle remodel itself and work better and to protect against abnormal heart rhythms. There is a wide variation in how severely the heart muscle is affected. How severe the problem is determines how badly you feel and how likely you are to recover with treatment. For this reason, it's very important to follow the instructions given to you by your OB or cardiologist.

Oh my gosh, now I'm scared there's something majorly wrong with me!

Please don't be. The conversations surrounding the rarer medical conditions in this book are not meant to induce fear or to make women afraid of having major medical problems. They are here to increase awareness of things we are often afraid to talk about. The aim is to help identify problems sooner so that the few women who are affected can get the care they need as early as possible.

Toolkit

Dealing with a major medical condition can change your world even more profoundly than giving birth. Here are a few strategies I recommend to help you process the changes and manage the emotional roller coaster. Even if you don't have health problems, these things will improve your ability to handle life's ups and downs.

Journal: Get a notebook you like and a special pen and start to write, dumping out everything that you're thinking and feeling. Also, make time and space at the end of the day to reflect on three things that you were grateful for that day. They don't have to be big things, but the act of doing this helps train your brain to notice the good things. It also reminds you of how blessed you are, even in this challenging season.

Get Outside: If you're physically unable to take a walk, drive to a park and sit on a blanket in the grass—or put one down in your own backyard. Breathe the fresh air, listen to the birds, and feel the breeze on your face. Run your hands through the grass, and hug a tree. In Japan they practice shinrin yoku—forest bathing—in which you go out into a forest and focus on the natural world around you with all five senses. If you are able to try this, it can bring a powerful sense of calm and peace.

Make a Good Playlist: Music is a powerful emotional trigger. Put together a short playlist you can turn on when you are feeling overwhelmed, and it will lift you up and give you strength.

Lean On Community: If you are part of an organized religion, lean into your faith group for support—both emotional and logistical. If your health allows, consider not only being a recipient of support, but giving support as well. Helping others is a powerful reminder of the blessings we have, even in difficult times.

Meditate: I found the idea of meditation very intimidating for many many years. My easily distractible, always-running brain resisted any attempt to just sit and be quiet. Once I started, however, it changed my world, and I've never stopped. There is no right or wrong way to meditate. It is often easier to start by finding music or a guided meditation online, but neither is required. Just find a comfy spot to sit, close your eyes, and breathe. Thoughts will come up; this is okay. Note what you thought about, and then set the thought aside for later and return to your breathing.

Baby Blues and Postpartum Depression

> "I've always been a pretty happy person, so I wasn't expecting the swirl of emotions after delivery. The mood swings that first week were overwhelming, one minute I was dancing with my baby, and the next I was a puddle of tears on the sofa. Nighttime feedings were the worst—I started streaming comedy shows to keep from getting caught up in anxiety. My mom came to stay with us for a few days to help me. After a week it started to get a lot better. My partner said my sunshine came back."
>
> —Kasie, 29, mama of one

What exactly are the "baby blues," and how are they different from postpartum depression?

The so-called "baby blues" are a cluster of mood changes occurring in the first couple of weeks after delivery, usually including anxiety, mood swings, crying spells, and overall sadness. Baby blues are very common and may affect up to 80% of parents. Yes, that's right—partners can get them, too! Medically speaking, the primary difference between baby blues and postpartum depression is duration. Baby blues, by definition, last up to two weeks. If your mood symptoms last at least two weeks, they meet the criteria to be considered postpartum depression.[1, 4]

Why do you get the baby blues?

Many factors go into the development of baby blues. The dramatic drop in estrogen and progesterone levels following delivery is thought to play a role in causing the baby blues. The cascade of powerful emotions that come with giving birth also contributes, as does the sheer exhaustion and life disruption from having a newborn. Some symptoms of the baby blues—decreased ability to concentrate, irritability, mood swings—are also seen with sleep deprivation. But whether the chicken or the egg came first doesn't change their existence. [1, 4]

Mood changes with major life events are very common. There's a whole set of mental health conditions related to this—they're called adjustment disorders. You can have depression symptoms, anxiety symptoms, or both. But the hallmark is undergoing a major life change and then developing symptoms. You have stress that is out of proportion to what is expected from an event and there isn't another explanation for it.[2]

I think of the baby blues as a kind of adjustment disorder. No matter how excited and happy you are about the birth of your baby, let's face it—your life is suddenly completely different from what it was just 24 hours beforehand. Some people cope with that okay. Others need time to process and adjust to the changes. Some of this is related to what your expectations were prior to your baby's birth, but it goes a lot deeper than that due to the physical and mental changes that happen to your body itself.

How do I cope with the baby blues?

The most important thing you can do is to connect with your support system. Talk about what is going on with the people you love and trust the most. See if they can help you create more time and space for self-care and rest. Being home alone with a newborn can be very isolating—and terrifying—especially for first-time mamas. Put your baby in the stroller and get out of the house. Drive to a coffee shop. Go wander around the mall. Take a deep breath, find your shoes, brush your teeth, and GO.

Enlist your partner, friends, and family to help you out. The physical exhaustion of being up and down all night feeding a newborn is real. Even if you are exclusively breastfeeding, having assistance with cooking, cleaning, and shopping allows you to sleep while your baby is napping. Think about your life before your baby for a moment. How tolerant were you at school or work the day after a late night out with friends? Getting enough sleep makes everything seem less challenging.

If you are having difficulty coping with daily tasks, please make sure to reach out to your doctor and get screened for postpartum depression. During the two weeks after delivery, you may meet the criteria for either condition (postpartum depression is sometimes referred to as "peripartum" depression because it can technically start before your baby is born). There is no tidy line between baby blues and postpartum depression. Think of it instead as a spectrum of severity. Getting assessed will help determine where you fall along that spectrum and whether you need additional assistance.

Does what I eat affect my mood?

What you eat can have a huge impact on your mood—and on your energy, too. Eating foods that supply you with a steady amount of energy throughout the day helps substantially with mood swings. What does this mean? It means sticking with foods that don't spike blood sugar, like lean proteins and complex carbohydrates. What proteins are considered lean? Unbreaded, skinless chicken on or off the bone, turkey (ground or whole), most cuts of pork, and many types of fish. Try to avoid processed proteins like hot dogs, ham, sausage, and bacon. The World Health Organization classifies both red meat and processed meat as group one carcinogens, meaning that they found enough proof in research that these foods can lead to colon cancer. Complex carbohydrates include oats, brown rice, legumes, and vegetables. It may feel weird to consider a bell pepper a complex carbohydrate, but, if you look at it on a basic level, the key difference between complex and simple carbohydrates is fiber. Most vegetables have a good amount of fiber relative to their overall calorie and carbohydrate content. Whole fruit (like an apple or a peach) and berries can also fall into this category, provided they're eaten in a reasonable quantity.

Foods that are high in omega-3 fatty acids, like nuts, seeds, and certain types of fish, lower inflammation in the brain and are believed to help with serotonin function, in addition to their well-known cognitive effects. Just be careful with fish, especially while breastfeeding, due to the potential for contamination with mercury and other heavy metals. Because one of the key amino acids for producing serotonin is tryptophan, foods that contain high levels of this amino acid, like turkey, chicken, and pumpkin seeds, may also be beneficial.

Over the last few years, an increasing amount of research has begun to link mental health conditions to problems with bacteria in the gut. If you have a history of irritable bowel syndrome or if you've taken a lot of antibiotics in your life, you may also get benefits from probiotics. Although these can be taken as supplements, getting them from fermented foods like pickles, sauerkraut, kimchi, and kombucha is preferred because they offer a wider variety of bacterial strains than most supplements. Research has shown that a diversity in gut flora is linked to better overall health, as well as the ability to maintain a healthy body weight. Other things that have been shown to help gut flora include a plant-based diet and certain types of intermittent fasting. While incorporating more plant foods and less animal foods is a good idea at almost every stage of life, intermittent fasting is not recommended during pregnancy or breastfeeding due to concerns for safety and impact on breast milk production.

"My fourth baby was different. With the first three, I don't think I even had the baby blues. But for whatever reason, when my fourth daughter was born, I developed severe depression. I didn't want to get out of bed, shower, eat, or do anything. I didn't even want to hold my own baby. It was awful. My husband was supposed to go back to work after a couple of weeks, and he ended up taking about two months of FMLA. I didn't want medication at first, but I could see the effect it was having on my other kids to see me the way I was. It ended up being the best decision ever. After a couple of weeks, I started to feel more human. I stayed on a low dose of medication for about six months, then tapered off and I've been fine ever since."

—Mary 32, mama of five

How is postpartum depression different from the baby blues?

There are several basic differences between the two conditions—though this is a spectrum and not two tidy disease buckets. First, postpartum depression lasts longer. Baby blues are transient; they go away after 10-14 days. Postpartum depression does not.

Second, postpartum depression symptoms are more severe. The lows are lower, the anxiety more pervasive, the overwhelm more dramatic. You may not want to get out of bed or do things you previously enjoyed. You may not eat as much—or you want to eat everything in sight.

Regardless of the exact symptoms you have, one of the hallmarks of postpartum depression is that your symptoms affect your ability to carry out the tasks of your day-to-day life. You struggle to function in some way. Often, you still do manage to function on some level, but it's hard. You must force yourself to do basic household tasks and care for yourself and your baby.

There is a short questionnaire that healthcare providers use to screen people for depression. These questions are included here to help you be more aware of what symptoms of depression can be. Some of them are obvious. For example, you feel a lot more sad than usual, or you just can't find the ambition to do anything. Others are much less obvious. I did not include the answer choices (various frequencies) or how to score the test, because although I am a doctor, I am not your doctor. My goal is simply to help you be more aware of what is going on with your body so that you can have the tools to get the help you need.

In the last two weeks, how often have you had:

1. Little interest/pleasure in doing things
2. Feeling down, depressed, or hopeless
3. Trouble falling/staying asleep or sleeping too much
4. Feeling tired or having little energy
5. Poor appetite or overeating
6. Feeling bad about yourself—or that you're a failure or have let yourself or your family down
7. Trouble concentrating on things, such as reading or watching television
8. Moving or speaking so slowly that other people could have noticed. Or the opposite—being so fidgety and restless that you have been moving around more than usual.
9. Thoughts that you would be better off dead or of hurting yourself

If you are answering things like "sometimes," "most of the time," or "almost always" to these questions (aside from #4 because we're all tired at this point), there is a good chance you do have some level of postpartum depression and that treatment would help you to feel better. This is especially true if the symptoms you are having are making it difficult for you to care for yourself and your family.

If you're struggling to get by or if you answered anything other than "never" to question #9, get help today. No delays, no "I'm just tired, it'll get better." Today. Pick up the phone and get a doctor's appointment. Be honest with your partner. Take a deep breath and be honest with your closest friends. This can feel really hard and scary, but it will help. After doing all that, make sure to look at the end of this chapter for more information on how to help yourself—even on the days when things feel overwhelming—and for information that your partner and friends can use to help you.[1, 3]

Are there things I can do that aren't medication? Are there vitamins or supplements I can take?

The most important things you can do for depression don't come in a bottle. Research shows that getting 30 minutes of daily exercise is just as effective as prescription antidepressants for people who have mild to moderate depression. You just had a baby so joining the local CrossFit gym is out, but most forms of low-to-medium intensity exercise are okay once your OB has cleared you for physical activity. And, walking is almost always allowed, so it's a good idea to check with your OB even before your postpartum visit if you'd like to be more active.

The second key is to get outside. If it's January in a cold climate, you may need to have someone watch your little one but going outside for at least 10-15 minutes can help improve your mood, energy, and sleep.

The third thing is connection. Working with a licensed mental health therapist can be an invaluable tool for balancing your moods and improving your coping skills. If you can't afford therapy or don't have access to mental health care, finding other moms can also create a support system of women who understand with your hospital, community center, or early education programs for a local mom's group can help give you that support system and keep you from feeling so isolated.

When it comes to taking an actual supplement, the number one thing to do is check with your pediatrician and make sure it is safe. Many effective over-the-counter supplements—including St John's Wort, one of the top-selling supplements for depression—are not safe for breastfeeding or certain medical conditions.

If you have low or low-normal levels, supplementing with vitamin D, B vitamins, magnesium, and zinc can help. Your doctor can check these levels with a simple lab draw. You can also get omega-3 fatty acids as supplements—either as EPA/DHA fish oils or as vegetarian formulations from algae. N-acetyl cysteine (NAC) is beginning to be studied in postpartum depression (including safety studies for lactation), but there are no safety studies for nursing, so this is an option only if you are not breastfeeding. SAMe, another popular supplement with some research support for benefits for depression, has not been studied in breastfeeding women, and therefore, is only an option if you are not breastfeeding.

What should I do? My brain hasn't felt like my own the last few days, and it's scary. Please help me!

Sometimes the chemical changes in your brain following having a baby can be profound enough to confuse your brain and start to go haywire. You may find yourself seeing and hearing things, only to discover a moment later that there's nothing there. You may hear voices even when you're alone. Thoughts that someone is coming to get you, someone is coming to steal your baby, or someone is watching you may cross your mind. Or you find yourself obsessing about keeping the house quiet, keeping germs away from your newborn, or repeatedly checking the doors. Sometimes you may even think of hurting yourself... or your baby.

These things are signs of postpartum psychosis, and they are very scary to experience. As the question above alludes, your brain is suddenly not your own, and reality is all messed up. There will be moments when things make sense and moments where nothing makes sense at all. If you've had any of the above, put down this book right now and find your partner or a friend immediately. If nobody is available, call your doctor's office or even 911. The symptoms you're having can come and go in an instant, and waiting to get help can have life-or-death consequences. If this sounds overly dramatic, understand that in this situation, your brain really isn't your own—it's been hijacked by things beyond your rational control.

This section is not meant to scare the 99% of women who don't need it. I included it because the information could save the life of the 1% of women who do. And even if it doesn't apply to you today, weeks or months down the road, you may encounter a mama battling postpartum psychosis. The knowledge you now have could help you save her life.[3]

My mom tells me to "get a grip" and that there's nothing wrong with me, which of course, makes me feel even worse. What should I do?

Having the baby blues or postpartum depression does not mean that you are weak, a bad mama, or an inferior human being. In fact, postpartum depression affects 17% of healthy women without a prior history of depression.[3] And those numbers go up when you look at women who have health problems or who gave birth to infants with health problems. That's nearly one in five women. And the prevalence of baby blues is even higher, affecting 39% of women in a meta-analysis performed in 2020.[4]

Despite the above evidence that these conditions are more common than perceived, many women feel alone and unable to talk to anyone about what they are experiencing. Scenarios like the one above contribute to these feelings. But times are slowly changing. One of the positive effects of the pandemic is the growing transparency and acceptance of mental health conditions.

Although you may continue to experience situations where you feel isolated or judged, supportive people are becoming easier to find. Women are more willing to talk about their experiences with postpartum depression (PPD), particularly to other women.

But how do you handle difficult situations when they do arise? What do you do with the unsupportive family member, the judgmental friend? There's no denying that it's tough to go through depression, and lacking social support makes it even tougher. First, check with your local hospital and with your doctor and see if there is a group for moms with PPD (or honestly, even just a group for new moms). If you find one, find a way to attend the next meeting. These types of groups usually allow you to bring your infant and will help you feel less alone.

Second, think about the people you know well. Identify at least one person in your life, ideally a female with children, that you think may be supportive of what you're going through. Pick up the phone and say, "Hey, I've been having a rough time since my baby was born. Do you have a minute to talk? I'd love to connect."

Third—and this one takes courage—look at the person invalidating your experience and say, "Hey. I love you, and I respect you. For me to be the best version of myself that I can be, I need you to support me and my current experience of motherhood. If you can't do that, then I can't spend time with you right now. My greatest priority now is caring for my baby and recovering my own health. I hope that we can reconnect down the road when things are easier for both of us." And leave it at that.

Motherhood of a newborn/infant is a special season, and though the days feel oh-so-long, they are gone in the blink of an eye. Due to their own issues or history, some people won't be able to walk down that road with you. And it's okay to let them go for this season. There are so many more people—women and men—who will understand and support you through the ups and downs of your journey of being a mama. Cultivate the relationships that bring you strength, help you to grow, and provide you joy. Let go of those that do not. Spend time with those who want to help you walk through depression and come out stronger, more beautiful, and more compassionate on the other side.

Toolkit

When you are struggling with depression and are overwhelmed, there are things you can do to help yourself build a path forward:

Create a routine. The brain loves patterns, it loves routines, it loves doing things on autopilot. Most babies also thrive with routines. So, create what feels like a doable initial daily schedule, and then start to follow it—a little bit at a time. Don't beat yourself up if you are five minutes off; use it as a basic "workflow" for your day. Knowing what comes next helps keep your brain out of stress and overwhelm.

Set tiny goals first. Like brushing your teeth or showering. Put on real clothes (not sweats and a baggy T-shirt) and makeup.

Reward yourself every time you do a goal or stick to an item in your routine. Nothing huge, just give yourself a smiley face or do a dance to a favorite song. If social media was your pre-baby jam, shoot an Instagram story about it. Celebrating your wins and rewarding yourself is a form of positive feedback. Rewards are much more motivating than fear.

You can also help your mind by helping your body:

Eat healthy. Healthy food gives you consistent energy to fuel your day and won't leave you crashing a couple of hours later the way candy bars will.

Avoid alcohol. Alcohol is a depressant. Even when mixed with caffeine, it still impacts your brain in a way you don't need. Drinking will not help you feel better.

Go for a walk. Aim for thirty minutes, preferably outside if the weather allows, at the best pace you can manage without going against any post-delivery restrictions your doctor has placed. Getting ready is hard. The first five minutes might be even tougher. But afterward, you will be so glad you did.

Start to incorporate some little things in your life that research has shown are beneficial for mental health:

Do something kind for someone else. It doesn't have to be formal volunteering. It doesn't even have to be big. Take a shot of a picture in a magazine that reminds you of a friend and text it with a note that says, "Thinking of you!" Bring up your neighbor's trash can. Treat the person in line behind you at the coffee shop. If you're not in a hurry, let someone check out ahead of you at the grocery store. Smile at the receptionist.

Listen to music that makes you happy. Background noise can have a surprisingly strong effect on mood. What's better for you and your baby—CNN with the latest disaster or the playlist from your wedding reception? Brownie points if you pick up your little one and dance along—double brownie points if you pick up your phone and take a silly selfie of the two of you and send it to your partner.

Get outside. Even if it's only as far as your own yard. If you're like me and you live somewhere that gets cold in the winter, seek out a local greenhouse or zoo with a tropics exhibit. If it's hot, find a shady area near the water to dip your toes in. You don't have to be outside for hours to feel the benefit—fifteen to thirty minutes is often enough.

Make human connections.

This one is usually the toughest because usually when you're depressed, you want to lay in bed and not see anyone. But one-on-one time with someone whose company you value can help.

- Try a support group for moms with postpartum depression.
- Make a date with a friend for a pedicure.
- Bring your baby and a magazine or book to a coffee shop.
- Sign up for Mommy and Me. Or enlist help from your circle and do a kid-free activity you enjoy.

Returning to Work... or Not?

"For the longest time, I thought I was weird. Like completely abnormal and weird. After my son was born, by the time my eight weeks of maternity leave was up—I had a c-section—I was so totally ready to go back to work. I felt like there was something wrong with me because I was completely over being at home with my baby. Not that I was excited to leave him at daycare with a stranger. I wasn't. I cried my eyes out. But I was going insane at home."

—Allie, 34, mama of two

"My whole life all I wanted to do was get married, have babies, and be June Cleaver. I think I was about six months along with our first baby when I told my husband that I didn't want to go back to work. It wasn't that my job was bad, don't get me wrong. Boss was okay, coworkers were okay. It was just that the career I wanted in my heart was being a homemaker."

—Jennifer, 36, mama of four

The above stories illustrate the two extremes of a common, and often emotionally charged, situation. Both women love their babies very much but have widely divergent personal career satisfaction needs. For women who did not work outside the home prior to delivery, the struggle to decide whether to return to work after giving birth doesn't typically exist unless something has happened to change the family's financial circumstances. But for women who have just had their first child, or for women who have been working and had one or more children in daycare, there is a decision to be made. They find themselves having to choose whether to be a full-time caregiver and homemaker, or whether to return to work on a full or part-time basis when maternity leave is over.

What does maternity leave look like in the U.S.?

Unlike most countries in the world, there is wide variability between employers surrounding maternity leave benefits. At the most restrictive, companies may offer no paid leave at all. At the most generous, companies may offer 8-12 weeks of at least partial pay, with the option to use additional vacation days. The most common situation is six weeks of full or partial pay after a vaginal delivery and eight weeks of full or partial pay after a c-section. A minority—but growing—number of employers are also offering between two to six weeks of paternity leave to partners. In most other developed countries around the world, maternity leave ranges from 3-12 months, typically with at least partial pay.

Financial issues aside, what else should I think about when deciding whether to return to my job after having a baby?

There are so many other things to consider when deciding whether to return to work when your maternity leave is up. Obviously, this is something that you and your partner will discuss together. But there is a certain degree of soul-searching that you will want to do—especially if both avenues are reasonably available to you.

First, you want to think about where you fall on the extrovert-introvert spectrum. If you tend to be more of a homebody and less of a social butterfly, it may not bother you to be home with your little one full-time. If you are very extroverted and love to be around people, then it will be harder to be home with your baby full-time unless you make a coordinated effort to get out of the house most days. If you're unsure where you fall on this spectrum, stop and think about how you felt during the beginning of the pandemic—the extreme case of staying home.

Second, think about how you feel about your current job. Do you like it? Why or why not? Do you like the place you work, the people you work with, the type of work you do? If you enjoy what you do and the people you work with, you may want to consider staying at your current workplace either full or part-time.

If you like the type of work you do but not your specific employer, then consider using the time off to help you explore job openings elsewhere. Or, if you like your specific employer but not your particular role, maybe there are internal openings that you could pursue.

Third, you want to think about how you feel about your field of work in general. If you don't like the type of work you do, having a baby is a natural break. You can consider taking a course in something new, pursuing a different line of work, or even an entirely new field. You can even start your own business. Although, you will be surprised by the amount of time you spend on basic household chores and caring for your baby, you will have some time in your day to work on these things—especially if you plan for them.

Fourth, consider how much of your personal identity is tied up in your career. I'm a doctor. It encompasses a big part of who I am and what I stand for. It isn't all of me, but it's a big part of my identity because of the years of life experiences it took to get there. Similar situations can be seen for careers in teaching, nursing, and law enforcement, and for women who were already business owners before becoming pregnant.

I work from home. Can I just keep my baby home with me?

Before the pandemic, I would've said absolutely not. Most companies prohibited this and required that you prove that you had another adult caring for your baby while you were working, regardless of the physical location of your baby.

In a post-Covid world, the answer is still probably not, but there are some companies that provide you with a degree of flexibility around having your children at home while you are working. But be prepared that this may come with a reduction in pay, as it's not possible to work full-time and care for an infant simultaneously, no matter how good of a multi-tasker you are.

If you are self-employed, it is technically possible to keep your baby at home and work. I say technically possible because whether or not it is feasible will depend on how many hours a day you need to devote to your business and what activities you need to do in order to keep your business up and running successfully.

I feel so guilty about leaving my baby in daycare while I'm at work!

> *"I cried so hard the first time I left my son at daycare. He was so tiny and helpless and I didn't want to miss a single minute. I'd love to say it got better after a few days, but it was at least three weeks before I could make the ten-minute drive to the office without tears."*
>
> **—Jennifer, 34, mama of one**

Even though it can be hard to see them, there are benefits to having your baby in daycare. The biggest one is socialization. We no longer live in large family groups, so children who attend daycare have more social stimulation than their counterparts. Along these lines, infants in daycare often develop language and communication skills earlier in life—particularly if your daycare emphasizes teaching these things. And when your child starts school, he/she will likely miss fewer days for illness than children who did not attend daycare. Whether these benefits outweigh the issues and emotional distress is an individual decision that only you can make.

Toolkit

Do I need to work? Make a financial spreadsheet.

There are two components to evaluating whether you need to return to work. The obvious one is financial. Can you balance your family budget without your income? Following is a list of expenses and considerations to think about as you evaluate your monthly income and expenditures.

1. How much money do you make every month after taxes?
2. What is the cost of daycare for your infant?
3. Whose job does your family carry health insurance through? If anyone is insured through your job, can you change to your significant other's insurance plan? What is the cost of doing so?
4. Looking at your family's finances, will you be able to maintain the financial ability to live congruent with your values? (Think of travel and other leisure activities, saving for college/retirement).
5. Is part-time work for your current employer a possibility?
6. Is there work in another field you could do on a part-time basis?
7. What is possible without putting undue stress on your family finances?
8. Also, consider how long you potentially want to stay home. Just for the first year? Until Kindergarten? Longer?

The second component is personal and looks at the intellectual, self-growth, and social aspects of being a working mom.

1. Rate how much you enjoy your current job from 1 to 10.
2. How intellectual are you? How much does your current work stimulate your mind? How much do you like to think and problem solve, or do mental puzzle-type activities?
3. How social are you? How much will you miss the social adult interactions throughout the day? Your baby, although adorable, is not a great conversationalist at this point. Are there local opportunities you would be able to pursue to prevent isolation?
4. How does your significant other feel about you staying home? Do they work from home or outside the home?

Options for childcare beyond traditional daycare centers:

- **In-home daycare**—instead of bringing your child to a large center, you go to someone else's house. Benefits include a smaller number of children, a more familiar style of setting, and lower cost. Drawbacks include fewer regulations and safeguards, and less consistent scheduling.
- **Nanny**—instead of bringing your child somewhere, why not bring the caregiver to the baby? A nanny shows up at your home each day and watches your child in your home. Many women who work from home will have a part-time or full-time nanny. Benefits include not having to pack and shuttle

your child around, and more individual attention. Drawbacks include a lack of backup for illness/vacation and the need to pay household worker employment taxes in most locations.

- **Au pair**—an au pair is a young foreign worker who comes to live with your family. Au pairs care for your children in exchange for room and board plus a stipend. Benefits include performance of care within your home, exposure to another language and culture, and flexible scheduling (up to 45 hours per week, 10 hours per day). Drawbacks include a loss of privacy, emotional investment, and communication barriers. Many au pairs also don't drive.

- **Babysitting cooperative**—an arrangement where multiple families agree to share childcare between themselves without any money changing hands, instead focusing on the exchange of points for care given and care received. Benefits include having your child develop closer social connections with a small group of peers, flexibility, and cost containment. Downsides include scheduling barriers, potential for unequal use, and lack of full-time availability.

Identity

"Around nine months postpartum, that time when things are usually going great, I started to feel profoundly stressed and unhappy. For days I couldn't figure out what was going on. Then I realized I don't even know who I am anymore. My whole life was taking care of my daughter and going to work. I'd pushed aside everything else I cared about and it was slowly eating away at me."

—Kathie, 26, mama of one

How does life change after having a baby?

Women have written whole books on this topic, but to put it simply, having your (first) baby creates a major change in your lifestyle. No matter how much you prepare for it, you'll still be surprised. Before your little one was born, life centered on friends, hobbies, work, and your significant other. After giving birth, your life feels like it's centered on just one thing—your baby.

For many women, their baby becomes their whole world, especially if it was difficult to get pregnant in the first place. Babies can be all-consuming. They can't do anything for themselves, and they'll let you know it. You can easily spend all your time caring for them and just enjoying their cuteness. You'll read books or blogs about how to care for them, join in-person and online moms groups, and take about a million pictures of them in all their moods. Your conversations will center around your baby, too. Because when they're first born, that's what your life is.

Even mamas who are having a second, third, or more baby will go through this, and it's a normal shift because of the effort involved in caring for a newborn. The difference with subsequent pregnancies is that you've already adapted to the mama role, you've already read the books and done the things. This doesn't make the time and mental investment any less, but it does make the shift easier. And when adding a younger sibling to your family, it is even more important to balance the new baby's needs with those of the rest of the family.

What are the benefits of being so absorbed in my baby?

No matter what you've heard, you can't give a baby too much love. That doesn't mean you should sleep with them, but it does mean that you should pick them up and cuddle them when they cry. Feelings of attachment and security form early and become underlying patterns for how your child responds to the word as he or she grows. Pay attention to your tone of voice, and to how you are feeling as you pick up your little one. If you feel anxious or stressed, your baby picks up on your feelings and unconsciously starts to perceive the world as an unsafe place. Now, does that mean every time you pick up your baby, you have to be happy? Of course not. That's ridiculous and unrealistic. But it does mean you want to be conscious of how you respond to your little one overall. Although they won't remember getting four immunizations at two months of age, it will neurologically imprint on them whether that moment of pain was followed by soothing and loving reassurance or by being strapped into their infant seat and rushed out the door, still screaming.

How much cuddling and attention your baby demands is influenced by their underlying temperament. Some babies are "easy," and others will scream day and night for no apparent reason. Most fall somewhere in between. My firstborn was a grumpy little guy who would sometimes cry for what felt like an eternity, no matter what I did. My second would take a nap even if he was starving, which I discovered only when he plummeted off the growth curve at four months of age—gulp! I remember being so jealous of friends who could do whatever they wanted, baby in tow. Then a friend loaned me her baby-wearing carrier. I had one but it made my shoulders hurt so badly. I discovered he was happy as a clam as long as he was snuggled up against me. He just needed to be close.

If you feel like your baby is more "challenging," pay close attention to what soothes them and what sets them off. See if the time of day matters. The late afternoon to early evening witching hour is real. Find ways to create more of what soothes them. Use your tribe if you need ideas and try new baby products or equipment before purchasing when you can. Lastly, although you want your newborn to be a large part of your world, remember that you don't want them to become your whole world to the exclusion of everything else.

Is it possible to be too focused on my baby?

Of course! Although this tiny human turned your world upside down, you still have interests, obligations, and an identity outside of being a mama. This is especially easy to forget for the first six months after having your first baby. When you're on maternity leave, your days are filled with your baby. Often the only adults you interact with are other moms or the clerk at the grocery store. Everyone else is working, and it's easy to let your whole world become being a mama.

That's fine for a while, but eventually, the pendulum swings back the other way for many women. This doesn't mean that you love your baby any less. It just means that you are more than your baby—more than just mama. You're a woman with goals, dreams, feelings, and interests that have nothing to do with your precious little one.

Although it may feel selfish, it's important to build in the "me time" when you can still do/have the things you enjoy—whether that's riding your bike, going to a movie, or being on a recreational sports team. Talk to your partner about setting aside time so you can go to dance class once a week, get your nails done twice a month, or whatever you enjoyed before your little one arrived on the scene. You won't regret it.

Why does self-care matters so much?

In the beginning, this may feel silly. You're riding the high of having a new baby. Even when you're physically exhausted from frequent feedings around the clock, you may not care because you're so wrapped up in loving your baby. But although this time is magical, it doesn't last forever. You can prolong the magic by taking steps to care for yourself from the beginning. Regular self-care prevents the burnout that inevitably follows from giving everything you have, all day every day, until you reach a breaking point.

> *"My husband was deployed when our daughter was born. He was able to come home for two weeks, and then he was gone. We didn't have family nearby and my friends all worked full-time, and many had kids of their own. Everyone kept telling me how amazing I was caring for a newborn on my own. They said what a wonderful mother I was. I felt like I was suffocating. Then one night my daughter wouldn't go back to sleep after eating at 3am. I was so exhausted I screamed at her, "Why won't you sleep—I hate you!" I started sobbing, too, picked her up, and cuddled her close in the recliner. Of course I didn't really hate her. I was being crushed under the pressure of trying to do it all."*
>
> **—Aimee, 26, mama of one**

I have patients and friends who've been Aimee. I've been her, too, which is why her story resonated so much with me. We all have our own internal breaking point, and having kids tends to expose our vulnerabilities. Taking the time for basic hygiene, rest, and the things that we value for ourselves goes miles toward improving our quality of life

What does self-care look like?

The exact items you choose will be as unique as your fingerprints. Usually, you will be able to identify at least one thing that you overwhelmingly desire. You have the thought, "I wish I could just ____" more than once a day. For me, that was going to the ice rink to skate. There were a lot of other things that sounded good—more than two hours of uninterrupted sleep, a massage, a rooftop happy hour with friends. But going to the rink was a deep emotional desire. I just wanted to feel like the me that I knew, the person I was before diaper changes and 2:00 am feedings took over my life. Pay attention to your thoughts over the next few days, and see if that phrase comes up for you, too.

Self-care items generally fall into a few categories. There are basic needs categories like showering in peace for as long as you want, eating a meal at the table that contains all the food groups, sleep, and exercise. There are traditional pampering activities like massage, a facial, and getting your hair or nails done. Then there are social activities like meeting friends for drinks, going to the movies, and shopping. Finally, there is hobby time, whether that's playing an instrument, physical activities like hiking/biking, artsy hobbies like drawing or making jewelry, or anything else that brings you joy that you used to do in your spare time—before your little one made spare time nonexistent.

What activity you choose matters far less than how much you are emotionally craving it. If you're doing well and a long way from burnout, the craving will be less intense. But it will still be there.

I encourage women to find one small thing they can do every day and to schedule one bigger thing each week. The small thing is often something you can incorporate into your day without assistance—like streaming an exercise video during naptime or splurging on fancy coffee. The bigger thing should involve a little planning and assistance from someone else—like making sure your partner will be home to watch the baby so you can take a dance class or meet a friend for happy hour after she gets off work. If your partner also looks a little frayed around the edges, consider asking grandma to watch your little one while the two of you go out for an early dinner at a favorite restaurant.

If you think going to happy hour with a friend seems selfish when you have a new baby, consider this: what matters most to your baby right now (aside from basic needs like food and safety) is love. It's hard to give the kind of loving care you want to when your own gas tank is empty. Just like the airplane message about putting on your oxygen mask before assisting others, you have to fill your own cup to have something to give those you love.

Help, I don't know who I am anymore!

Me neither. Having a baby—especially your first baby—creates upheaval in your life. Day-to-day life changes dramatically. The things you do are different. The things you think about are different. Even the people you spend your time with can become different. Many women gravitate towards hanging out with other women with infants or small children because they can commiserate on shared experiences. You are all in the same season of life, and it's easy to create connections through common ground.

The challenge is that at some point between nursing, diapers, and mom-talk, the part of you that got shoved into a dark corner starts to cry out, "What about me?!"

"Mama" may be the primary identity you are currently living, but it isn't your only one. Before having children, I defined myself as an adult figure skater, a hiker, an avid gardener, and a writer. How did you define yourself? And have you engaged in any of those passions since your baby was born?

For many women, the answer is not at all or only rarely. It's easy to do. We're hardwired to care for others. But the challenge lies in doing so without losing all of the other pieces of who we are at our core. Neglecting who you are deep inside will not bring you long-term joy. It'll bring plenty of internal resistance, underlying frustration, and often a little bit of sadness.

"Before my daughter was born, I would go to open mic nights a couple nights a week to share my poems with my writer friends. The first month I was so wrapped up in Olivia that I didn't even know what night it was. But then a writer friend came by to see her, and I realized how much I missed writing poetry. Of course, my first poems were all about her cute little self. I had to ask my mom to watch Olivia for open mic night—my husband works evenings. I procrastinated for weeks, but when I finally asked she was so nice about it that I wished I had done it sooner."

—Jessica, 33, mama of one

Please don't feel guilty and selfish about honoring the parts of you that make you who you are. Doing the things that make you happy and whole will make you a better parent, and most of the time, the people in your life are happy to support you. That doesn't necessarily mean you should be doing this all the time, however. There's a difference between honoring yourself and trying to hang on to a season of life that you're no longer living. Embrace your current reality. Take advantage of the different circumstances to try something you've always wanted to do but didn't fit into your old single life. Enroll in an online art class, learn a foreign language, or take up knitting.

Are there resources you recommend on how to be a good mom?

More than a decade ago, a patient asked me this question. She wasn't asking because she was unsure about how often to breastfeed or bathe her baby. Here's the gist of what she said when I asked her to clarify what she meant.

"There's so much stuff out there. Some of it says to do this. Some of it says to do that. My mom says one thing, my mother-in-law another. It's all so confusing, and I really want to do it right, and I just don't know what to believe anymore!"

In this age of technology, we are drowning in information. One of the biggest challenges is that there's nobody out there reviewing the content for accuracy. This is true for any industry, not just being mama. So, how do we know what's right? Is it possible for more than one opinion to be true?

There's so much pressure in our society to be a good mom, but there's no clear definition of what "good" really is. Courtesy of social media, we're reminded a million times a day of everyone else's ideas—yet we rarely take time to sit down, reflect, and define our own. What constitutes being a good mama is going to be different for everyone. What a baby needs to grow and thrive is going to be different for different infants. Things that constitute abuse aside, under the giant umbrella of options, there is a path that is right for you and your baby.

So there are two things you have to do. The first is to determine what being a "good mom" looks like to you. This will end up being a combination of living your life in alignment with your values and what you instinctively feel is right for your baby (and subsequently is demonstrated to work). It's okay if your path is different from that of your friends. We all have different lives and different babies, and there's no right answer for everyone.

The second is to take a deep breath and start to respond differently to the noise around you. If someone suggests something, smile and say, "Thank you for sharing your experience with me. I appreciate your advice." And then change the topic or move on in the conversation. If the advice is not aligned with your values, discard it as someone else's truth that is not true for you. If it seems to be aligned with how you want to show up each day, do some research, try a test run, and see what you think. Remember that just because you try something doesn't mean you have to keep doing it forever. Just like going shopping, put the clothes on, look in the mirror, and see if it fits who you are and the kind of mom you choose to be.

Toolkit

Five inexpensive options for pampering yourself:

- Shower/bath with scented candles
- Do your own manicure/pedicure
- Pick up an at-home facial mask
- Take a walk in nature
- Get that bottle of lotion that reminds you of the beach

Five questions to help you pick a new hobby to try:

- What have I always wanted to learn?
- Do I want to get out of the house or do it from home?
- What do people say I have a knack for doing?
- What did I secretly love as a kid but was too scared to admit?
- Do I want to be up on my feet or sitting quietly?

Five things to consider when looking at self-care activities:

- Can it be done from home or will I need to go somewhere?
- Can I do it whenever I choose or does it happen at a set time?
- Do I need someone to watch my baby?
- Am I physically/mentally capable of pursuing this right now?
- Will it bring me joy?

You're Gonna Miss This

As I write this, my youngest is almost three. As much as I love watching his little personality develop, a part of me wants to turn back the clock to the days when he was snuggled close to me. My oldest is now in kindergarten, and my godson just became a teenager. They say that the days go slow, but the years go fast, and it's so true.

If you're up every hour or two with a newborn, in a few months, your baby will start sleeping more at night and, thankfully, so will you. If your toddler is a ticking time bomb of tantrums, know that his brain is changing so fast and before you know it, he'll be starting school. And if your teenager is being stubborn and moody, remember that before you know it, she'll be graduating from high school and off on her own.

There will be things you don't miss, like wearing maxi pads for weeks on end after delivery, the nipple pain during those first weeks of breastfeeding, and sleepless nights walking the floor with a colicky baby. But these things quickly fade, and you'll be left with warm, fuzzy memories of newborn cuddles and toddler excitement.

I was blessed to have the opportunity to be home more when my boys were very young. Working evenings and nights in urgent care gave me the chance to watch my oldest son grow up minute by minute. Yes, there were days when I envied my friends who could take a day off work, bring their kids to daycare, and have a few hours of peace and quiet to accomplish things. But those same friends also envied me and my ability to trade part of my income to be home with my baby. We all did what worked for us. If there's one thing that almost two decades in medicine has taught me, it's that what works for one person doesn't necessarily work for another.

Motherhood is a journey of seasons, with the newborn season fading into the infant season fading into toddlerhood and beyond. When a season gets tough, you can remind yourself that these days will not be here forever. And when the days are good, I try to capture and savor every minute. Small children live only in the moment with very little sense of the passage of time. One of the most powerful skills you can gain from being a mama is the ability to live in the "Now" with them—even for just a few moments. When you're done, the grown-up world will still be there.

Creating a good, solid morning routine that can carry you through will make a big difference in your ability to care for yourself and your family during the day. For example, if you have diastasis, plan 10-15 minutes to do your exercises before the craziness of the day begins. If you want time to journal, pray, exercise, or even just drink a cup of coffee and savor the silence, these are things worth getting up for. The key is thinking about what you need in order to show up as the person you want to be. Your routine may change as your kids leave babyhood behind, but preserve that little piece of the day for you and you only.

It is my hope that this book has empowered you by giving you an understanding of what happens to your body after pregnancy and childbirth. In many circles, discussing "female problems" is still taboo. Too many times, I've heard my patients start a sentence with the words, "There's this one thing I've had for a long time…"

The information I've included is but a small portion of the growing resources out there for new mamas. Many of these resources are developed by women for women, and mamas supporting mamas. When you're overwhelmed and sleep-deprived, the results of a Google search can be so intimidating. I wanted to give you a place to start and the knowledge and support to help you find your own best path. We are all on the same journey, but no two roads are the same. We are strongest when we can support and learn from each other.

It's an amazing gift that our bodies can nurture, grow, birth, and then sustain a tiny baby. And that process forever changes us physically, mentally, and emotionally. As women, we don't all share the same details of motherhood, but we all share in the collective story of Becoming Mama.

To everything, there is a season. Embrace the journey. Lead with your heart.

With love from my home to yours…

References

Santa Claus Belly

1. Pullar, Juliet M et al. "The Roles of Vitamin C in Skin Health." Nutrients vol. 9,8 866. 12 Aug. 2017, doi:10.3390/nu9080866
2. Zinder, Roman et al. "Vitamin A and Wound Healing." Nutrition in clinical practice : official publication of the American Society for Parenteral and Enteral Nutrition vol. 34,6 (2019): 839-849. doi:10.1002/ncp.10420
3. Matts PJ, Oblong JE, Bissett DL. A review of the range of effects of niacinamide in human skin. Intl Fed Soc Cosmet Chem Mag. 2002; 5: 285–289.
4. Dermatol Surg. 2005 Jul; 31(7 Pt 2): 860-5; discussion 865 Niacinamide: A B vitamin that improves aging facial skin appearance. Bissett DL, Oblong JE, Berge CA. www.ncbi.nlm.nih.gov/pubmed/16029679.
5. Geesin JC, Darr D, Kaufman R, Murad S, Pinnell SR. Ascorbic acid specifically increases type I and type III procollagen messenger RNA levels in human skin fibroblast. J Invest Dermatol 1988; 90: 420-424. (PubMed).

When Giving Birth Involves Surgery

1. Chen MD, Katherine. "Postpartum Endometritis." UpToDate. 23 May 2024. https://www.uptodate.com/contents/postpartum-endometritis#:~:text=This%20topic%20last%20updated%3A%20May%2008%2C%202023.&text=Postpartum%20(puerperile)%20endometritis%20refers%20to,after%20cesarean%20than%20vaginal%20birth.
2. Larsson C, Djuvfelt E, Lindam A, Tunón K, Nordin P. Surgical complications after caesarean section: A population-based cohort study. PLoS One. 2021 Oct 5;16(10):e0258222. doi: 10.1371/journal.pone.0258222. PMID: 34610046; PMCID: PMC8491947.

Diastasis Recti

1. Cavalli M, Aiolfi A, Bruni PG, Manfredini L, Lombardo F, Bonfanti MT, Bona D, Campanelli G. Prevalence and risk factors for diastasis recti abdominis: a review and proposal of a new anatomical variation. Hernia. 2021 Aug;25(4):883-890. doi: 10.1007/s10029-021-02468-8. Epub 2021 Aug 6. PMID: 34363190; PMCID: PMC8370915.
2. Michalska A, Rokita W, Wolder D, Pogorzelska J, Kaczmarczyk K. Diastasis recti abdominis—a review of treatment methods. Ginekol Pol. 2018;89(2):97-101. doi: 10.5603/GP.a2018.0016. PMID: 29512814.
3. Jessen ML, Öberg S, Rosenberg J. Treatment Options for Abdominal Rectus Diastasis. Front Surg. 2019 Nov 19;6:65. doi: 10.3389/fsurg.2019.00065. PMID: 31803753; PMCID: PMC6877697.
4. "Diastasis Recti" The Cleveland Clinic. 8 Feb 2022. https://my.clevelandclinic.org/health/diseases/22346-diastasis-recti

Yikes, I Just Wet My Pants

1. Ghaderi F, Oskouei AE. Physiotherapy for women with stress urinary incontinence: a review article. J Phys Ther Sci. 2014 Sep;26(9):1493-9. doi: 10.1589/jpts.26.1493. Epub 2014 Sep 17. PMID: 25276044; PMCID: PMC4175265.
2. Parente, M P L et al. "The influence of an occipito-posterior malposition on the biomechanical behavior of the pelvic floor." European journal of obstetrics, gynecology, and reproductive biology vol. 144 Suppl 1 (2009): S166-9. doi:10.1016/j.ejogrb.2009.02.033

It's All Falling Out

1. "Pelvic Organ Prolapse." NHS Choices, NHS, 24 Mar. 2021, www.nhs.uk/conditions/pelvic-organ-prolapse/

Hair Loss

1. Choi, Sekyu et al. "Corticosterone inhibits GAS6 to govern hair follicle stem-cell quiescence." Nature vol. 592,7854 (2021): 428-432. doi:10.1038/s41586-021-03417-2
2. Guo EL, Katta R. Diet and hair loss: effects of nutrient deficiency and supplement use. Dermatol Pract Concept. 2017 Jan 31;7(1):1-10. doi: 10.5826/dpc.0701a01. PMID: 28243487; PMCID: PMC5315033.
3. "Pregnancy and Hair Loss." American Pregnancy Association. https://americanpregnancy.org/healthy-pregnancy/pregnancy-health-wellness/hair-loss-during-pregnancy/#:~:text=Telogen%20effluvium%20is%20the%20excessive,during%20pregnancy%2C%20it%20is%20temporary.

4. "Hair Loss: Who Gets and Causes." American Academy of Dermatology Association. https://www.aad.org/public/diseases/hair-loss/causes/18-causes

5. Salinas M, Leiva-Salinas M, Flores E, López-Garrigós M, Leiva-Salinas C. Alopecia and Iron Deficiency: An Interventional Pilot Study in Primary Care to Improve the Request of Ferritin. Adv Hematol. 2020 Aug 26;2020:7341018. doi: 10.1155/2020/7341018. PMID: 32908518; PMCID: PMC7471793.

6. Treistr-Goltzman Y, Yarza S, Peleg R. Iron Deficiency and Nonscarring Alopecia in Women: Systematic Review and Meta-Analysis. Skin Appendage Disord. 2022 Mar;8(2):83-92. doi: 10.1159/000519952. Epub 2021 Nov 19. PMID: 35415182; PMCID: PMC8928181.

To Nurse or Not to Nurse—That is the Question

1. Stevens EE, Patrick TE, Pickler R. A history of infant feeding. J Perinat Educ. 2009 Spring;18(2):32-9. doi: 10.1624/105812409X426314. PMID: 20190854; PMCID: PMC2684040.

2. Zakarija-Grkovic I, Stewart F. Treatments for breast engorgement during lactation. Cochrane Database Syst Rev. 2020 Sep 18;9(9):CD006946. doi: 10.1002/14651858.CD006946.pub4. PMID: 32944940; PMCID: PMC8094412.

Coping With the Exhaustion

1. Institute of Medicine (US) Committee on Sleep Medicine and Research; Colten HR, Altevogt BM, editors. Sleep Disorders and Sleep Deprivation: An Unmet Public Health Problem. Washington (DC): National Academies Press (US); 2006. 2, Sleep Physiology. Available from: https://www.ncbi.nlm.nih.gov/books/NBK19956

2. Moon, Rachel Y et al. "Sleep-Related Infant Deaths: Updated 2022 Recommendations for Reducing Infant Deaths in the Sleep Environment." Pediatrics vol. 150,1 (2022): e2022057990. doi:10.1542/peds.2022-057990

Beyond Exhaustion

1. Huang GY, Zhang LY, Long-Le M A, Wang LX. Clinical characteristics and risk factors for peripartum cardiomyopathy. Afr Health Sci. 2012 Mar;12(1):26-31. PMID: 23066416; PMCID: PMC3462514.

2. Mubarik A, Chippa V, Iqbal AM. Postpartum Cardiomyopathy. [Updated 2023 Apr 16]. In: StatPearls [Internet]. Treasure Island (FL): StatPearls Publishing; 2023 Jan-. Available from: https://www.ncbi.nlm.nih.gov/books/NBK534770/

Baby Blues and Postpartum Depression

1. Balaram K, Marwaha R. Postpartum Blues. [Updated 2023 Mar 6]. In: StatPearls [Internet]. Treasure Island (FL): StatPearls Publishing; 2023 Jan-. Available from: https://www.ncbi.nlm.nih.gov/books/NBK554546/
2. "Adjustment Disorders." Mayo Clinic. 6 July 2023. https://www.mayoclinic.org/diseases-conditions/adjustment-disorders/diagnosis-treatment/drc-20355230
3. Shorey, Shefaly, et al. "Prevalence and incidence of postpartum depression among healthy mothers: A systematic review and meta-analysis." Journal of psychiatric research 104 (2018): 235-248.
4. Rezaie-Keikhaie, Khadije, et al. "Systematic review and meta-analysis of the prevalence of the maternity blues in the postpartum period." Journal of Obstetric, Gynecologic & Neonatal Nursing 49.2 (2020): 127-136.

Acknowledgements

Thank you to Jodi, my friend and chiropractor, for your support during my own post-birth recovery and for telling me to write this book in the first place. Without you, the idea that grew into *Becoming Mama* would not exist.

Special thanks to my fellow "writing moms," Concetta, Emily, Johanna, and Megan whose encouragement and feedback along the way was invaluable.

To Jess at Two Penny Publishing, for putting up with all of my delays and disasters and helping me get through the messy middle of real life and make it through to the finish line.

And last, but perhaps most importantly, thank you to all of the women who've shared their stories of laughter and heartache. This book belongs to you—to all women everywhere who've traveled the journey of Becoming Mama.

About The Author

Michele Brezinski, MD, is a board-certified family medicine physician trained in integrative, functional, and lifestyle medicine. She has over fifteen years of clinical experience in both inpatient and outpatient settings. Michele is a mama to two adorable sons. She loves  writing and teaching and supports expanded access to lifestyle medicine for the traditionally underserved. She also speaks on stress-related illness and overcoming chronic stress, and she advocates for holistic care for working mothers.